A 1908 milk train headed by **Behemoth**
P J R Reed collection

GREAT WESTERN RAILWAY

SIPHONS

An account of vehicles built for milk traffic

on the

Jack N Slinn

With drawings by

Bernard K Clarke

CONTENTS

ISBN   0   902835   10   6

Designed by Peter Esgate

Printed in England by J B Shears & Sons Ltd, Basingstoke

© 1986 J. Slinn/B. Clarke/HMRS and those
persons/organisations credited.

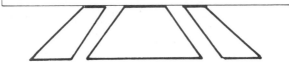

PREFACE

This book endeavours to set out the history of the vans code named SIPHON built by the Great Western Railway and the Western Region of BR ostensibly for the carriage of milk traffic.

It is based on the outline story recently printed by the Historical Model Railway Society in its *Journal* and it includes all the information that I have been able to uncover. It cannot pretend to be complete but it assembles more information about these vehicles, in one place, than most earlier accounts.

The book would not have got off the ground but for the willing co-operation of Bernard Clarke whose excellent drawings impelled me into re-writing the original text.

I am indebted to others for help in tracing the development and history of the vans and my appreciation of their help is more fully set out at the end of the volume.

JACK N SLINN
Woking
1986

INTRODUCTION

It would appear from the Company's rolling stock records that there was negligible demand for special vehicles or arrangements for the carriage of milk until well into the second half of the nineteenth century. This is, of course, not unexpected when one considers the social conditions of the times. Cities and towns were smaller than perhaps we realise and cows could be kept within easy reach for delivery of milk by horse and cart. When Paddington station was built it was on a green field site and outside of London the transport problems were even less pressing.

Another feature of the times was the private enterprise shewn by inhabitants of the towns who kept cows in their back yards. A report of the Departmental Committee on Milk and the Milk Industry (CMD 1854 of 1923) in a brief historical section revealed that in addition to the farm lands on the periphery of towns this was a flourishing trade. Even as late as 1865 there were 40,000 of these stall-fed beasts in London alone.

The industrial revolution meant that towns rapidly increased in size and presumably the demand for milk increased in proportion. This report goes on to state that the milk industry owed its start and growth entirely to the rise of the railways.

The earliest date noted in Great Western records of specific milk vehicles is in 1870 and by this time the narrow gauge was preponderant but the first note of vans allocated or branded for milk traffic was on the Broad Gauge. The vans so traced are outlined in Appendix 1 for interest.

Milk obviously has to be moved fast before it deteriorates and it follows that vehicles to carry it had to be capable of transit in passenger trains for the freight of the period would never have coped. This passenger rating lasted throughout the whole era of rail milk traffic. When the traffic began it was obviously of no great magnitude and could well be accommodated by conversions of existing stock; all the Broad Gauge milk vans were conversions.

Within a few years, however, the demand was such that the railways had to make special efforts to cope. The Great Western apparently decided that all such traffic should go Narrow Gauge although the Broad Gauge conversions lasted into the late 1880s.

This book, therefore, restricts itself to a consideration of the purpose built milk vans built for the Narrow Gauge all of which in due course acquired the code name

SIPHON. For ease of reference to the various designs it has been set out in sections covering the various code names rather than in strict chronological sequence. It is interesting that a complete series of Diagram Numbers (the O series) was set aside for milk vans by the Company. These were allocated about 1910 and the existing vehicles were given Diagram numbers with an O prefix in roughly the order of building. Details of Diagrams and their numbers are listed under each type.

It only remains in this section to deal with the one Narrow Gauge conversion that has been traced. In July 1866 a batch of open carriage trucks was supplied by the North of England Wagon Company and one of these is noted in the Company's Carriage Truck Register as "converted to covered milk — date unknown". It could well be that this was the first step to devising a purpose built milk van; there are no clues as to its appearance other than the recorded dimensions.

NG Conversion

Built OCT	OCT No	To Milk	Cond	
7/66	62	?	10/79	15ft 6in × 7ft 6in × 6ft 6in high. 4 wheels wheelbase 9ft

These preliminary notes have dealt with the precursors to the proper milk vans which now follow in sections ordered as above.

Plate 1   GWR
A train of empty Siphons about to leave Paddington in 1923 behind **Wynnstay**. The vehicles reading back from the loco are: PBV No 274 (V3), Siphon O.2, PBV (V4), Siphons O.4, O.8 O.2 (ex-Scorpion) two more of O.2 and O.5

FIRST FOUR WHEEL DESIGN

Plate 2   **London Transport**
A four wheel original Siphon with the later style of door framing

Once the Railway had decided to construct milk vans which were for that traffic only
it set to with a will and within two years out of a total production of 70 of the 4 wheel
type, 60 were running.

The appearance of these vans was completely different from anything then owned
by the Company although the conversion of carriage truck No 62, described in the
Introduction, may possibly have been similar. In place of the close boarded covered
vans and the wooden and windowed passenger brake and luggage vans these milk

3

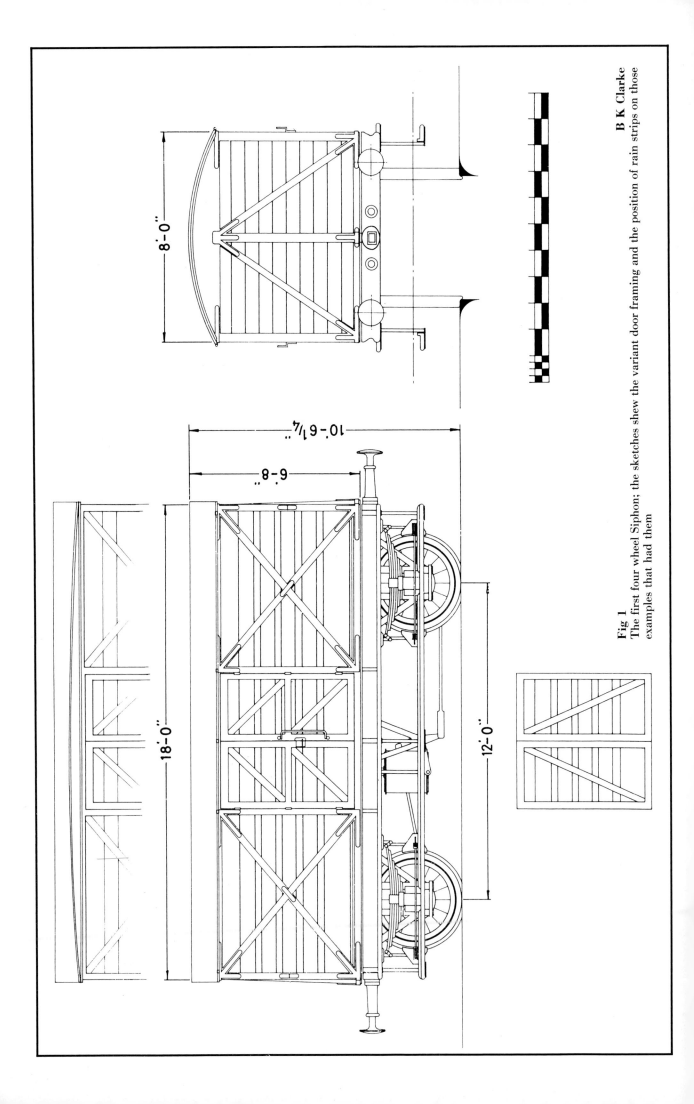

8'-0"

10'-6 1/4"

6'-8.9"

18'-0"

12'-0"

B K Clarke

Fig 1
The first four wheel Siphon; the sketches shew the variant door framing and the position of rain strips on those examples that had them

Plate 3
The earlier pattern of door framing on the first Siphons The accident is at Yetminster

vans were made with planking with wide gaps between each plank. This style of construction was to last until the longer bogie designs were introduced many years later.

This feature was obviously influenced by the need to ensure adequate ventilation and the necessity to keep the temperature of the load as low as possible. It is quite an elegant solution to the problem as it economises in the cost of the body and the speed of the train guarantees a free flow of cool air through the gaps in the body side.

The drawings and the illustrations adequately cover the general appearance of the vehicles but one or two points are worth emphasis. The first two Lots built had the doors framed in two halves which, at first glance, gave the appearance of opening in two parts and one van was actually modified so that the bottom half of the door dropped down as a flap while the upper half opened as two cupboard doors. This was undoubtedly a trial to see whether a drop flat would facilitate loading of churns and it is surprising that it was not apparently found useful. At any rate it was the only such conversion. The last Lot of this design carried the diagonally braced "one-piece" door which was to become the standard for all the non-bogie Siphons.

The load of these vans was originally 4 or 5 tons with 6ft springs but some with altered springing, possibly to the 4ft 6in type, were upgraded to 7 tons. Lot 180, still with 4ft 6in springs, was built to carry 5 tons. All these were fitted with clasp type brakes with the rigging outside the axleboxes. Automatic vacuum brakes were added in the 1880s.

5

As first built these Siphons had footboards below the doors only but between 1886 and 1888, in common with other passenger stock, lower footboards were added at axlebox height to run the length of the body and the footboards at solebar level were also extended to the same length.

The livery of these short vans when built would be the small G.W.R. and although no photographs have yet been found which shews this, it is almost certain that, like the later 6 wheel types, the Company letters and the serial number were painted on the plank second from the top of the body side. Tare and load were probably at either end of the bottom plank. When the large letters "G" and "W" were introduced in 1904 there were enough survivors for the standard modification used on the 6 wheel Siphons to be applied. This involved filling in the gap between the bottom two planks within the lower triangle formed by side bracing with an additional short plank to cope with the size of the letters. One would have expected that a sheet of thin wood within this space would have been adequate and cheaper. Finally between 1905 and 1907 steam pipes were added to these vans which enabled them to be marshalled anywhere within a passenger train.

LOT 85

Built	No	Cond	Built	No	Cond	Built	No	Cond
1/73	319	4/99	4/73	329	11/00	5/73	339	11/99
	320	5/05		330	5/02		340	10/04
4/73	321	9/10		331	5/99		341	5/10
	322	11/08		332	7/11		342	7/11
	323	8/05		333	7/04		343	8/05
	324	12/04		334	1/10	4/73	344	5/02
	325	11/08		335	8/00		345	6/01
	326	8/05	5/73	336	6/01	5/73	346	5/02
	327	11/11		337	9/13		347	11/99
	328	9/98		338	6/00		348	7/11

NOTES
No 346 altered to have half depth top doors and a lower drop down flap in 6/87

LOT 132

Built	No	Cond	Built	No	Cond	Built	No	Cond
12/74	420	7/99	12/74	430	9/96	12/74	440	9/13
	421	6/10		431	7/04		441	9/10
	422	11/11		432	10/82		442	10/12
	423	7/04		433	8/14		443	6/01
	424	7/00		434	11/11		444	7/11
	425	1/13		435	11/11		445	8/99

426	5/14		436	1/13		446	7/11
427	2/04		437	11/11		447	1/13
428	2/99		438	10/09		448	1/04
429	1/13		439	9/13		449	11/12

NOTES
No 429 had steam pipes fitted 11/06
No 440 allocated to the Old Milford branch train 9/03

LOT 180

Built	No	Cond	Built	No	Cond	Built	No	Cond
2/78	510	3/11	3/78	513	5/14	3/78	517	8/05
	511	3/11		514	11/11		518	9/97
	512	9/10		515	9/10		519	10/12
				516	4/04			

NOTES
No 510 branded Return to Swansea Dock 1/09 and fitted with "Wood wheels"
No 516 marked as 4 ton and fitted continuous footboards 7/86

Any of the above that lasted after about 1910 were allocated to Passenger Diagram
O.1 for which there was a Swindon ¼in diagram numbered 35041

SIX WHEEL SIPHONS

Before considering each of the six wheel Diagrams separately it is helpful to outline some general notes about the class as a whole and to provide some definitions of terms which will recur in the narrative.

Between August 1879 and the end of 1904 34 Lots were raised and 629 vans were constructed to this basic design and it is inevitable that, over such a period and considering the numbers involved, there were obvious, if minor, differences in their appearance.

Originally these Siphons were constructed for milk traffic but it soon became apparent that they were suitable for other traffic. There had always been a fair amount of fish traffic and these vehicles were an obvious candidate to be used for this. Fish, in casks or crates was packed in ice which melted en route giving the problem of disposing of the water that then accumulated. With the Siphons that were designated as "Fish" this was accommodated by raising the centre of the floor to give natural drainage.

The differences to the naked eye concerned the shape of the roofs, the height of the body and the number of side double doors. Roofs followed the pattern of contemporary passenger coaches the earliest building having "Arc roofs" which were the contour of a simple arc of a circle. Later models had the "three-centre roof' where the larger central portion comprised an arc of a large radius circle while the two edge sections, over the eaves, were arcs of much smaller radius; the drawings make this much clearer than any words but the terms are a useful shorthand.

Although the overall length remained basically constant later designs had three double doors each side while the earlier ones had but two and the final version had end doors also. Body heights increased over the years and ranged from 6ft 4½in to 7ft 6in but the large majority were 6ft 8in. The very lowest were on conversions from open carriage trucks; these had a slightly lower profile to the Arc roof.

The final allocation of the different types to Diagram Numbers was slightly anomalous as it upset the chronological sequence. When the type was first introduced the survivors of the four wheeled vans had already been placed on Diagram O.1 so it was natural that any following milk vans should be Diagram O.2. This, indeed, was what was done. But when a slightly different design came to be introduced this too became Diagram O.2. The anomaly of this struck the authorities and to cure this the original O.2 allocation was split when the last of the four wheel vans disappeared and Diagram O.1 became available. Surprisingly, however, the later batch of the six wheel version was the subject of the transfer to Diagram O.1.

The table below gives a summary of the final Diagram allocation and the salient differences between them:

Diagram	Roof Type	Doors	Body Height	Notes
0.1	3-centre	2	6ft 8in	Some 6ft 4½in
0.2	Arc	2	6ft 8in	
0.3	3-centre	2	6ft 8in	
0.4	3-centre	3	6ft 8in	
0.5	3-centre	3	7ft 6in	
0.6	3-centre	3	7ft 6in	End doors also

It seems the anomaly of different types on the one Diagram O.2 had been spotted even before the Diagram O.1 became available for a drawing has been seen at Swindon endorsed Diagram O.1[1].

As indicated in the Introduction the various types are discussed below in the Diagram order set out above rather than in strict chronological sequence.

Diagram O.1

With the increasing traffic building of Siphons continued from 1879 with a bigger and better design. Mention has already been made of the necessity for fast transport of milk and, in the 1870s, the GWR had determined on a standard for passenger coaches of 6 wheels for main line duties and 4 wheel for branch and surburban work. It was natural, therefore, that any improved milk vans should adopt the 6 wheel standard. The first design to this new standard, as stated earlier, ultimately became Diagram O.2 while the second batch, the construction of which started in 1889, was Diagram O.1.

Overall dimensions, which were basically standard for all the 6 wheel versions, were 27ft 6in length and 8ft wide and 19ft wheelbase. In common with coaches of the period the roof contour was the 3-centre type but the outside appearance of the ends of the vans followed the design of the Arc roof specimens in having the supporting beam immediately below the roof of a deeper section than later examples, with its bottom edge parallel to the floor.

The four Lots on this Diagram had what the Lot book refers to as deep loop sticks to support the roof internally. Later designs had combination roof sticks which were apparently stronger but of thinner section. This marginal decrease in internal capacity may have been the reason for the allocation of these Lots to Diagram O.1 rather than chronological allocation which seems to be the more obvious solution.

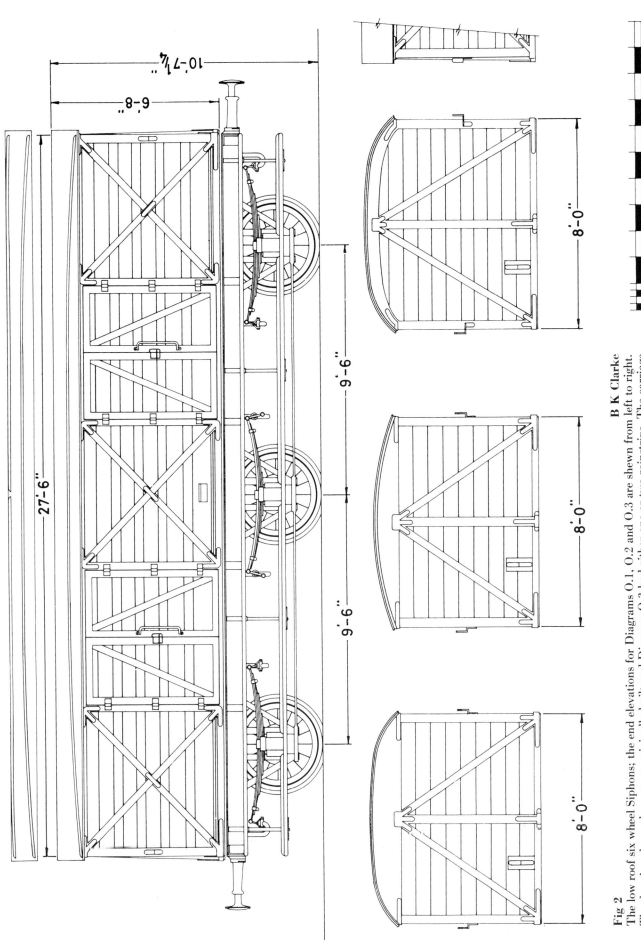

10'-7 1/4"
6'-8"
27'-6"
9'-6"
9'-6"
8'-0"
8'-0"
8'-0"

B K Clarke

Fig 2
The low roof six wheel Siphons; the end elevations for Diagrams O.1, O.2 and O.3 are shewn from left to right. The drawing shews the vans as originally built and Diagram O.3 had either one or two rainstrips. The carriage truck conversions had a flatter arc roof and clasp brakes as in Diagram O.1

Plate 4
No 734 (O.1) and No 1797 (O.4) in nineteenth century lettering style with G.W.R. on top plank

This Diagram, too, saw the first recognition of the use of Siphons for fish traffic, three out of the four Lots being designated as suitable for either traffic. By the turn of the century it occurred to the authorities that Siphons were versatile enough not to be restricted to Milk and Fish but were eminently suitable for other perishable goods. Photographs exist which shew their use to convey strawberries and flowers landed from the Channel Islands at Weymouth.

These vans were fitted with either side hand brakes between 1909 and 1917 but in later years some of these fittings were removed. Lots 486 and 535 were fitted with steam pipes between 1903 and 1906 and the load was increased from 6T to 10T in 1905. In common with other stock continuous footboards were added from 1889.

LOT 486

Built	No	Cond	Built	No	Cond	Built	No	Cond
7/89	697	5/37	8/89	714	5/32	3/90	730	6/34
	698	4/32		715	10/46	2/90	731	3/34
	699	6/38		716	11/32		732	5/37
	700	11/32	12/89	717	4/39	1/90	733	6/34
	701	8/33		718	5/36		734	12/38
	702	5/37		719	2/35	2/90	735	5/33

Built	No	Cond	Built	No	Cond	Built	No	Cond
	703	4/38		720	10/29	3/90	736	6/34
	704	6/36		721	8/36		737	5/36
	705	10/39		722	6/34		738	2/33
	706	12/32		723	11/31		739	5/33
8/89	707	2/35		724	10/31		740	6/34
	708	10/39		725	12/35		741	4/36
	709	2/32		726	12/31		742	2/33
	710	5/36	2/90	727	10/34		743	11/32
	711	11/35		728	5/36		744	12/38
	712	11/31		729	11/36		745	6/38
	713	8/31					746	5/36

The first 20 vans were Milk Vans while the last 30 were designated as Fish Vans; for differences see text.

Plate 5
No 1992 with the 16in G W lettering

L E Copeland

LOT 535

Built	No	Cond	Built	No	Cond	Built	No	Cond
4/90	951	1/34	4/90	958	6/34	6/90	964	3/33
	952	11/32		959	11/35	7/90	965	10/33
	953	5/36		960	6/32	6/90	966	12/27
	954	11/37	5/90	961	6/36		967	6/32
	955	1/40	7/90	962	6/34		968	10/33
	956	12/35	6/90	963	9/38	7/90	969	2/32
	957	4/38				6/90	970	6/32

This Lot was designated as Milk Vans

LOT 547

Built	No	Cond	Built	No	Cond	Built	No	Cond
8/90	971	5/36	8/90	979	12/36	9/90	988	12/35
	972	11/31	9/90	980	11/26		989	5/35
	973	7/35		981	6/33	10/90	990	7/32
	974	1/37		982	7/32		991	11/26
	975	2/33		983	6/34		992	8/33
	976	4/33		984	9/32		993	11/32
	977	5/32		985	7/31		994	12/26
	978	6/36		986	2/32		995	5/32
				987	12/38			

This Lot was designated Milk and Fish Vans

LOT 690

Built	No	Cond	Built	No	Cond	Built	No	Cond
3/93	1991	10/32	3/93	1994	7/35	3/93	1998	9/39
	1992	2/33		1995	3/35		1999	2/32
	1993	10/39		1996	10/34		2000	9/32
				1997	9/37			

This Lot was designated as Milk Vans

Plate 6   NUVB
Interior of the first 6 wheel Siphons shewing the roof bracing

Diagram O.2

This Diagram accommodates the first batches of six wheel Siphons built. The success of the earlier 4 wheel type and the increasing traffic impelled the Company to embark upon a large and continuing programme of milk van construction. As told already in the section on Diagram O.1 contemporary practice was to build main line passenger rated stock with six wheels and these were the first of this design. They did, however, continue former practice in having Arc roofs.

The framing and general appearance, apart from the roof profile, was similar to Diagram O.1 but there were minor differences between the Lots of this Diagram. The purpose built vans were all 6ft 8in high in the body but wheelbases differed. Lot 189 was 19ft whereas Lots 217 and 278 had theirs reduced to 18ft.

In addition to the new built stock there were conversions from open carriage trucks. The first of these on Lot 357 was seemingly a prototype. An early casualty among the former 4 wheel Siphons was No 432 and to replace this a new body was made for a spare carriage truck frame. Everyone must have been happy with the outcome as, later, the whole of Lot 268, built as Carriage Trucks was altered to Siphons. It is not recorded which carriage truck was the guinea pig and a search by elimination through the stock register was not successful; it might have been a Broad Gauge conversion to narrow gauge of 1878 but the Broad Gauge Registers are silent on the dimensions.

Plate 7   Kidderminster Library
No 547 before 1904 with number on top plank and G.W.R. on the next to bottom plank

14

The conversions of the Carriage Trucks of Lot 268 provided two different types of body. A batch of 6, listed in the table as "high body", were 6ft 8in high while the remainder were 6ft 4½in. The "prototype" on Lot 357 was also the lower 6ft 4½in.

The rebuilds could be recognised by the outside clasp brake linkage and an apparently slightly lower radius arc roof. All Lots had their load increased from 6T to 10T in 1905.

LOT 189

Built	No	Cond	Built	No	Cond	Built	No	Cond
8/79	520	11/28	10/79	523	2/31	10/79	527	5/31
10/79	521	12/31	9/79	524	12/28		528	5/32
	522	1/30	10/79	525	11/26		529	9/28
				526	9/31			

NOTES
This Lot has "Wood wheels" — presumably Mansell type?

Plate 8   J P Richards
No 656 in 16in standard G W lettering

LOT 217

Built	No	Cond	Built	No	Cond	Built	No	Cond
5/81	530	3/28	6/81	537	6/95	7/81	543	7/31
	531	9/31		538	8/27	5/81	544	8/34
6/81	532	11/28	5/81	539	12/29		545	2/32
7/81	533	10/30		540	12/29		546	5/36
5/81	534	5/31		541	7/29		547	7/29
6/81	535	6/28	6/81	542	10/29	7/81	548	7/29
	536	4/27				6/81	549	2/82

NOTES

No 536 damaged by the Southern Railway who paid compensation

No 537 Written off as Engineers' conversion

LOT 278

Built	No	Cond	Built	No	Cond	Built	No	Cond
6/83	601	12/28	9/83	611	11/37	12/83	621	7/32
	602	1/35		612	12/32		622	5/37
	603	9/32	10/83	613	2/31		623	2/31
	604	4/33		614	2/31		624	10/30
10/83	605	2/31		615	7/31		625	9/31
	606	8/31		616	11/91		626	6/34
	607	2/32		617	11/26		627	10/30
	608	5/32		618	9/31		628	4/31
9/83	609	8/31		619	5/31		629	8/30
	610	6/32		620	8/30		630	7/32

NOTES

No 603 written "Load to be evenly distributed" 5/17

No 604 fitted with shelves for strawberry traffic 7/02; branded Return to Rossett

No 606 fitted with shelves for strawberry traffic 6/06; branded Return to Rossett

No 605 fitted with blackboards each side. Presumably as an experiment for chalking on loading details.

LOT 268

This Lot was issued for Open Carriage Trucks which were built. Without the issue of a further Lot Number these were converted to Milk Vans.

Built	OCT No	Siphon No	Date	Cond
12/84	53	691	6/88	2/29
	1	692	6/88	5/32
11/84	69	693	8/88	10/31
12/84	9	694	10/88	2/33
	312	695	11/88	7/32
	74	696	12/88	10/31

The above were vans with high body and 18ft wheelbase

Built	OCT No	Siphon No	Date	Cond
12/84	41	647	10/86	10/31
	25	648	11/86	1/30
	34	649		4/35
	32	650		1/34
	55	651	12/86	1/31
	35	652	11/86	2/32

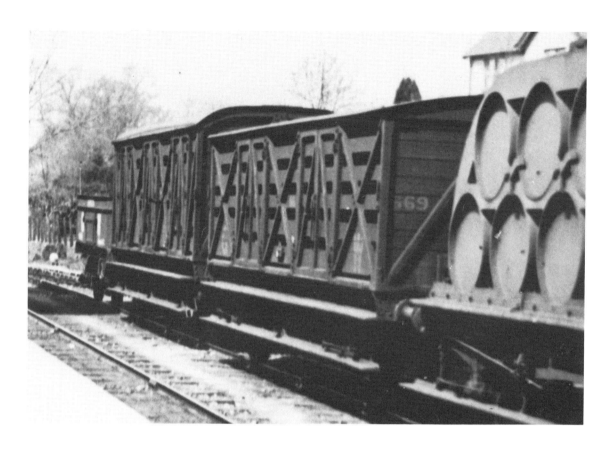

Plate 9   S M Davey
No 669 of the Arc roof type; one of those converted from carriage trucks

	73	653	6/34
	314	654	12/86	11/31
	64	655	1/31
	67	656	11/86	11/31
	33	657	6/28
	52	658	12/86	10/31
10/84	72	659	12/28
11/84	6	660	1/87	5/33
12/84	45	661	11/26
	19	662	12/86	3/29
	80	663	5/37
	36	664	6/36
	48	665	12/31
	37	666	2/32
	76	667	12/31
	70	668	1/87	6/28
	75	669	6/30
	81	670	8/31

The above were vans with low body and 19ft wheelbase

NOTES
No 693 fitted with shelves for strawberry traffic 6/06
No 662 fitted with shelves for Rossett strawberry traffic 6/06

LOT 357

Built	No	Cond
5/86	432	12/29

This was a replacement for the 4-wheel Siphon condemned in 1882 of the same serial number

All these were on Passenger Diagram O.2 for which the Swindon ¼in Diagram Number was 35042

Diagram O.3

Construction of two door milk vans with 6ft 8in high bodies continued after the introduction into traffic of the last of Diagram O.1 and there were only minor differences in appearance to be observed.

Mention has already been made of the "combination roof sticks" with which the vans on this Diagram were fitted. From the exterior of the van this alteration in design was seen in the supporting member across the end immediately below roof level. This was now much shallower and its bottom edge followed the contour of the 3-centre roof instead of being parallel to the floor as previously.

All these were new built and all had 19ft wheelbase and their load was 6T later increased to 10T.

LOT 710

Built	No	Cond	Built	No	Cond	Built	No	Cond
11/93	1951	4/36	12/93	1964	4/34	2/94	1978	9/37
	1952	6/36		1965	5/36		1979	6/33
	1953	12/38		1966	9/38		1980	12/38
	1954	9/37		1967	9/37		1981	6/38
	1955	7/36		1968	9/36		1982	4/36
	1956	12/38		1969	7/39	3/94	1983	8/27
	1957	5/32		1970	7/39		1984	9/38
	1958	9/37		1971	11/36		1985	12/36
	1959	4/36		1972	7/39		1986	10/39
	1960	9/37		1973	9/37		1987	10/35
	1961	9/37		1974	11/37		1988	11/37
	1962	10/48	2/94	1975	9/36		1989	9/37
12/93	1963	4/34		1976	4/36		1990	9/37
				1977	5/36			

The Vans in this Lot were fitted with either side brake gear between 1909 and 1917. Some fittings were later removed. They were designated as Milk Vans.

Plate 10
No 1990 in weather beaten livery in 1930

F W Hutton-Stott

LOT 741

Built	No	Cond	Built	No	Cond	Built	No	Cond
11/94	1901	12/36	12/94	1918	12/36	4/95	1934	6/51
	1902	6/36		1919	6/36		1935	6/47
	1903	9/37		1920	11/29	3/95	1936	10/46
	1904	6/36	2/95	1921	10/52		1937	9/34
	1905	6/38		1922	9/35		1938	11/38
	1906	6/33		1923	5/36	4/95	1939	3/47
	1907	5/32		1924	6/47		1940	10/47
	1908	6/36		1925	8/54	5/95	1941	8/48
	1909	11/37		1926	11/37		1942	2/37
	1910	7/27		1927	7/29		1943	12/29
12/94	1911	4/39		1928	1/46		1944	6/33
	1912	7/35		1929	1/16		1945	8/51
	1913	5/36		1930	9/38		1946	9/37
	1914	4/39	3/95	1931	11/47		1947	8/47
	1915	6/36		1932	3/46		1948	3/48
	1916	8/48	4/95	1933	4/34		1949	12/26
	1917	1/40					1950	12/28

No 1929 was involved in the Warminster accident

The underframe of No 1931 was used for tank truck No 39882 in 12/47

Nos 1921, 1932 and 1935 were fitted with roof brackets in 9/32 to carry headboards "RABBIT TRAFFIC HELSTON TO SHEFFIELD". These were removed after a couple of years when the traffic ceased to be remunerative with improving economic conditions. Designated Milk Vans

No 1925 branded "Penzance" in 3/25

LOT 770

Built	No	Cond	Built	No	Cond	Built	No	Cond
12/95	1891	10/46	12/95	1894	10/40	12/95	1898	6/40
	1892	2/31		1895	4/49		1899	10/48
	1893	10/39		1896	3/48		1900	10/36
				1897	1/46			

This Lot designated Milk Vans

The Siphons with two side doors and three-centre roof profile were finally identified by two Diagram Numbers. While any of the four wheel Siphons existed the vans of Lots 486, 535, 547 and 690 were allocated to Passenger Diagram O.1[1] and this was ultimately numbered Diagram O.1. Lots 710, 741 and 770 were on Passenger Diagram O.3. The differences are outlined in the text.

For Diagram O.3 the Swindon ¼in Diagram number was 35043

Plate 11   Source unknown
No 1528 with vestiges of a "shirt button" monogram still just visible

20

Diagram O.4

The six wheel Siphons had obviously proved their worth and the Traffic Department had found them generally useful. Apparently it had been found that only one milk churn at a time could be got through the doors so the next batch was modified to have three double doors each side, of slightly less overall width, instead of the two of previous designs. This meant more staff but in those days men were cheap; the cynic might well ask why the need for extra speed in loading when station stops and transit times on the Railway were more than generous.

Dimensions had now become standard at 6ft 8in body height, 27ft 6in long 8ft wide and 19ft wheelbase and all the O.4 Diagram except Lot 930 were originally identical. This Lot used up second hand underframes which were in stock so there were varying lengths and wheelbases; the table gives all the details.

Two kinds of modification to individual vans should be noted. No 1777 was repaired in 1907 and the opportunity was taken to close board the sides half way up and to surmount these with louvre ventilators as on the contemporary Siphon Cs. With the latter being then built it was probably easier to effect a major repair in this fashion as the parts were readily available.

No 1000 was another with a variant repair. It is recorded as being fitted with half boarded sides but no dates are quoted in the Van Register.

All the relevant details are in the table and there is nothing to add except to remark in passing that this Diagram has the largest number of vehicles in the non-passenger carrying stock lists.

Plate 12   F W Hutton-Stott
This shews the loading of churns one upon another in No 1654 in 1930

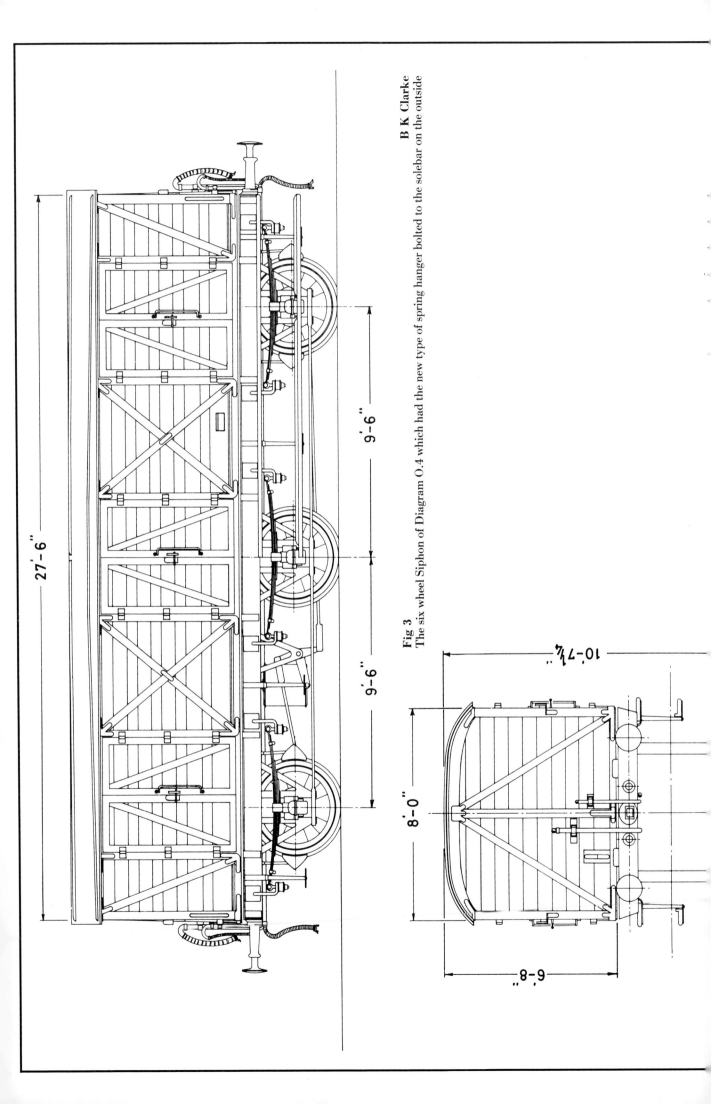

27'-6"

9'-6"

9'-6"

8'-0"

10'-7¾"

8'-9"

Fig 3
The six wheel Siphon of Diagram O.4 which had the new type of spring hanger bolted to the solebar on the outside

B K Clarke

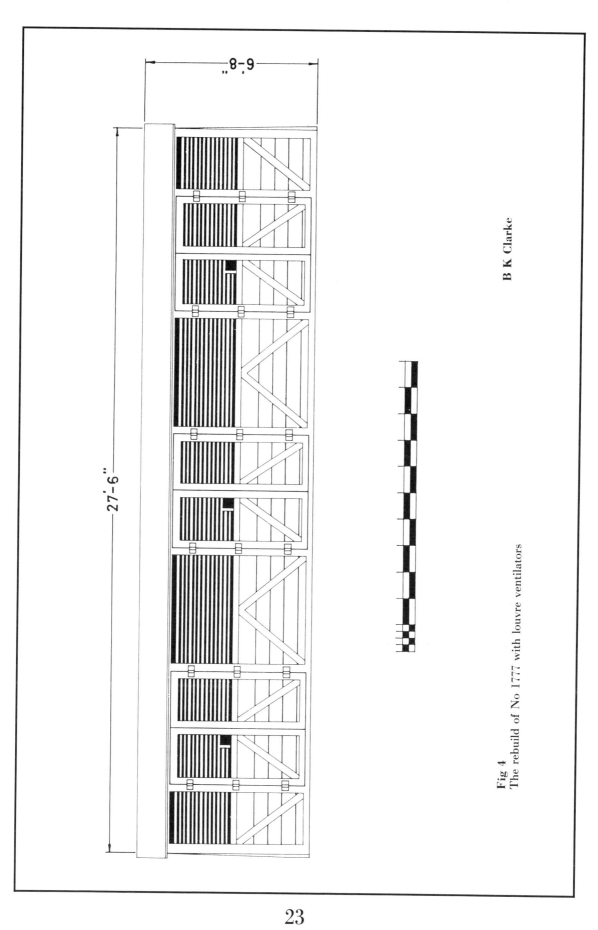

8'-9"

27'-6"

B K Clarke

Fig 4
The rebuild of No 1777 with louvre ventilators

LOT 788

Built	No	Cond	Built	No	Cond	Built	No	Cond
2/96	1879	6/33	2/96	1882	11/47	2/96	1886	3/46
	1880	4/34		1883	3/47		1887	1/48
	1881	2/52		1884	9/31		1888	4/46
				1885	1/46		1889	9/35
							1890	

LOT 800

Built	No	Cond	Built	No	Cond	Built	No	Cond
4/96	1869	5/36	6/96	1872	4/51	7/96	1876	6/46
6/96	1870	10/56		1873	4/34		1877	3/49
	1871	2/32		1874	10/49		1978	10/46
				1875	11/26			

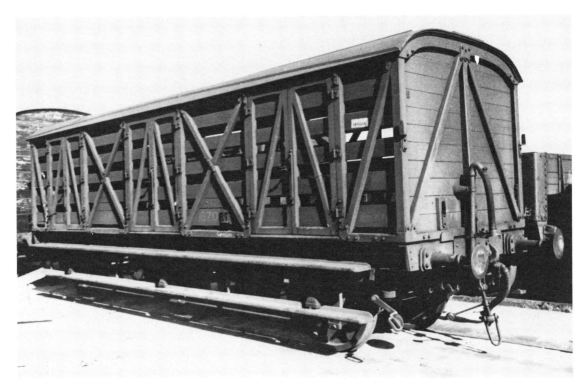

Plate 13   **M Longridge**
No 1870 of Diagram O.4 shortly after Nationalisation. This shews the double rainstrips and the block upon which
the tail lamp bracket was mounted. It still carries the either side brake

LOT 822
Westinghouse pipes

Built	No	Cond	Built	No	Cond	Built	No	Cond
11/96	1859	3/46	11/96	1862	12/26	11/96	1866	3/47
	1860	10/42		1863			1867	11/32
	1861	1/37		1864	9/31		1868	3/47
				1865	9/31			

LOT 825

Built	No	Cond	Built	No	Cond	Built	No	Cond
10/96	1853	6/33	10/96	1855	8/29	10/96	1857	10/49
	1854	9/35		1856	3/48		1858	3/47

LOT 835

Built	No	Cond	Built	No	Cond	Built	No	Cond
5/97	1843	4/51	5/97	1846	5/54	5/97	1850	12/26
	1844	4/37		1847	10/46	6/97	1851	12/29
	1845	5/48	6/97	1848	3/46	5/97	1852	6/47
			5/97	1849	7/56			

LOT 848
Dual fitted Vacuum and Westinghouse Brakes

Built	No	Cond	Built	No	Cond	Built	No	Cond
7/97	1823	3/46	7/97	1830	2/47	8/97	1836	7/29
	1824	3/55		1831	6/39		1837	8/48
	1825	3/47		1832	3/46		1838	9/35
	1826	6/51	8/97	1833	10/46		1839	12/38
	1827	8/36		1834	7/47		1840	10/46
6/97	1828	3/48		1835	8/50		1841	12/27
7/97	1829	5/36					1842	3/47

LOT 856

Built	No	Cond	Built	No	Cond	Built	No	Cond
12/97	1793	2/30	12/97	1796	9/35	12/97	1800	6/33
	1794	10/47		1797	9/39		1801	4/34
	1795	8/48		1798	9/35		1802	6/33
				1799	11/27			

LOT 857
Dual fitted Vacuum and Westinghouse Brakes

Built	No	Cond	Built	No	Cond	Built	No	Cond
12/97	1813	6/47	12/97	1816	12/28	12/97	1820	12/38
	1814	6/28		1817	10/47		1821	11/47
	1815	8/50		1818	4/32		1822	4/36
				1819	3/47			

LOT 868
Dual fitted Vacuum and Westinghouse Brakes

Built	No	Cond	Built	No	Cond	Built	No	Cond
3/98	1803	11/47	3/98	1806	11/45	3/98	1810	6/31
	1804	12/50		1807	7/32		1811	4/48
	1805	3/48		1808	10/27		1812	10/48
				1809	8/50			

Plate 14   **D M Lee**
An unidentified Siphon of Diagram O.4 sold out of stock. With the removal of the footboards the axlebox and truss rod detail is revealed

LOT 880

Built	No	Cond	Built	No	Cond	Built	No	Cond
5/98	1783	10/47	6/98	1786	7/50	6/98	1790	3/46
	1784	3/28		1787	3/49	5/98	1791	8/51
	1785	7/47	5/98	1788	8/35		1792	4/46
				1789	10/37			

LOT 942
Dual fitted Vacuum and Westinghouse Brakes

Built	No	Cond	Built	No	Cond	Built	No	Cond
4/00	1773	10/46	5/00	1776	6/47	4/00	1780	3/46
5/00	1774	3/28		1777	10/47	5/00	1781	10/47
	1775	10/47	4/00	1778	3/46		1782	11/29
				1779	4/34			

LOT 943

Built	No	Cond	Built	No	Cond	Built	No	Cond
6/00	1739	6/47	6/00	1742	3/49	6/00	1746	8/31
	1740	5/49		1743	8/55		1747	7/50
	1741	10/46		1744	4/51		1748	6/48
				1745	6/33			

LOT 951
Dual fitted Vacuum and Westinghouse Brakes

Built	No	Cond	Built	No	Cond	Built	No	Cond
11/00	1753	1/48	11/00	1760	9/49	3/01	1766	11/46
	1754	9/31		1761	3/28		1767	10/35

Built	No	Cond	Built	No	Cond	Built	No	Cond
	1755	11/45		1762	2/49	2/01	1768	12/50
	1756	7/32	2/01	1763	3/47		1769	1/46
	1757	6/53	3/01	1764	11/45		1770	2/37
	1758	7/49		1765	11/45	3/01	1771	7/51
	1759	12/36					1772	9/38

LOT 961

Built	No	Cond	Built	No	Cond	Built	No	Cond
12/00	1719	10/46	11/00	1726	9/48	1/01	1732	8/50
	1720	8/47	12/00	1727	4/34		1733	11/28
	1721	11/27		1728	8/50	12/00	1734	3/49
	1722	7/46		1729	7/29		1735	5/27
	1723	9/38		1730	9/50		1736	10/48
11/00	1724	3/48		1731	6/43		1737	10/47
	1725	3/47					1738	9/51

LOT 979

Built	No	Cond	Built	No	Cond	Built	No	Cond
6/01	1709	3/46	6/01	1712	11/45	7/01	1716	11/45
	1710	11/45		1713	11/26		1717	10/32
	1711	6/32		1714	12/47		1718	3/49
			7/01	1715	11/45			

LOT 993

Built	No	Cond	Built	No	Cond	Built	No	Cond
5/02	1689	11/45	5/02	1696	11/45	6/02	1702	9/48
	1690	4/49		1697	5/49		1703	10/47
	1691	7/47		1698	10/46	5/02	1704	11/45
	1692	8/54	6/02	1699	2/49		1705	4/32
	1693	11/47		1700	11/47	6/02	1706	11/45
	1694	6/33		1701	9/48		1707	12/47
	1695	12/47					1708	2/37

LOT 997
Dual fitted Vacuum and Westinghouse Brakes

Built	No	Cond	Built	No	Cond	Built	No	Cond
8/02	1664	3/46	8/02	1672	2/51	9/02	1681	1/46
	1665	3/52		1673	11/45	10/02	1682	11/26
	1666	4/32	9/02	1674	1/46		1683	2/37
	1667	8/47		1675	7/51	9/02	1684	3/46
	1668	5/31		1676	1/37		1685	6/33
	1669	4/46		1677	3/47		1686	7/48
	1670	8/50		1678	8/27		1687	2/53
	1671	6/47		1679	3/46		1688	3/47
				1680	7/51			

LOT 1016

Built	No	Cond	Built	No	Cond	Built	No	Cond
12/02	1644	4/51	11/02	1651	5/46	1/03	1657	8/50
	1645	12/28	12/02	1652	3/46		1658	7/51
	1646	10/46		1653	10/47		1659	10/46
	1647	1/48		1654	10/46		1660	9/48
	1648	11/45		1655	11/45		1661	10/46
11/02	1649	3/47		1656	6/33		1662	12/36
	1650	1/51					1663	10/45

LOT 1034

Built	No	Cond	Built	No	Cond	Built	No	Cond
5/03	1634	11/47	5/03	1637	3/47	5/03	1641	8/50
	1635	9/31		1638	10/46		1642	8/47
	1636	1/37		1639	10/46		1643	10/47
				1640	3/47			

Of the above LOT 997 is recorded as a Milk and Fish Van. The others are Milk Vans.

LOT 930
Built on second-hand underframes with various dimensions

Built	No	Cond	Dimensions	Wheelbase
12/99	616	8/47	27ft × 8ft	18ft 6in
	996	10/46	27ft 11in × 8ft	18ft
	997	5/36	27ft 11in × 8ft	19ft
	998	1/40	27ft 11in × 8ft	18ft
	999	2/32	27ft 11in × 8ft	18ft
	1000	2/32	27ft 11in × 8ft	18ft
	1749	12/48	27ft 11in × 8ft	19ft 6in
	1750	10/42	27ft × 8ft	18ft 6in
	1751	8/51	27ft 11in × 8ft	18ft
	1752	5/48	27ft × 8ft	18ft 6in
			All 6ft 8in high	

All the above Lots were on Passenger Diagram O.4 for which the Swindon ¼in Diagram Number was 12704

NOTES
No 1826 had its body removed and the underframe was used as a match truck at Barry Dock, No DW 159

No 1881 was sold on condemnation in 2/52

No 1860 had its underframe renewed using the one from No 523 of LOT 189

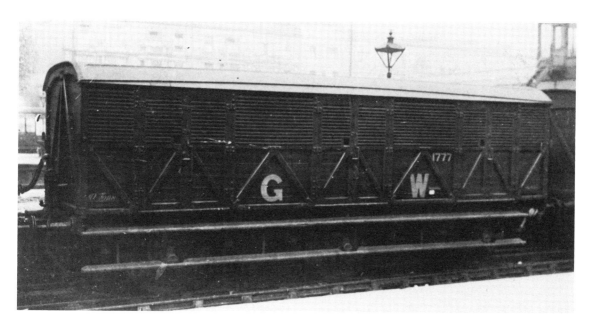

Plate 15   **F W Hutton-Stott**
The Siphon rebuilt with deep louvres, No 1777, seen at Addison Road in 1930

No 1830; the underframe of this one was used in the construction of tank truck No 39882

No 1811; the underframe of this one was used in the construction of tank truck No 39945 in 6/48

No 1777 was repaired in 4/07 and fitted with half boarded sides and louvre ventilators

Nos 1664 and 1686 were branded at some time (probably when new) "FOR FISH TRAFFIC ONLY" but this was soon obliterated

No 1659 was branded "TO WORK BETWEEN BISHOPS CLEEVE AND BIRMINGHAM ONLY in 11/18

Roof brackets to carry destination boards with the legend "RABBIT TRAFFIC HELSTON TO SHEFFIELD" were fitted as below and the vans were marked "via Banbury" after 9/31
No 1842 in 9/31, No 1863 in 9/31, No 1668 in 9/29, No 1681 in 8/36 No 1792 in 9/29 and Nos 1884, 1679, 1680, 1649 and 1640 during 1931/2

No 1850 fitted with shelves for strawberry traffic 1/21

No 1839 fitted with roof board brackets 9/27

No 1745 branded Return to Rossett

No 1687 branded Lifton & Paddington 9/50

No 1000 is recorded as having half boarded sides but no date is known for the alteration.

Lot 825 had Westinghouse pipes only but the dual fitted Lots after this had both vacuum and Westinghouse brakes. Steam heating pipes were added after Lot 868 and the original load was 6T later increased to 10T.

Plate 16   G Y Hemingway
One of Diagram O.4, believed to be No 1792, fitted with roof brackets for destination boards

Plate 17   G Y Hemingway
A three quarter view of what is believed to be No 1792 (Diagram O.4) shewing the shape of the roof brackets

30

Diagram O.5

After so many built to standard dimensions over the previous seven years there was a change in 1903 when this Diagram was introduced with bodies now 7ft 6in high. It does not seem to be recorded in official vehicle histories but, as both Lots were designated Fish Vans, the enhanced height was possibly to enable fish crates or barrels to be stacked better. The original height already provided for the stacking of milk churns one upon the other.

Another feature of these two Lots was that all were fitted with both vacuum and Westinghouse brakes which made them much more useful in transits to other railways and obviated transhipments between vehicles at the exchange stations. Steam pipes were fitted.

Finally one of the last Lot was rebuilt with end doors to be in all respects similar to those on Diagram O.6 and was so re-classified.

LOT 1039
Dual fitted Vacuum and Westinghouse brakes

Built	No	Cond	Built	No	Cond	Built	No	Cond
8/03	1609	11/45	9/03	1617	4/48	10/03	1626	1/37
	1610	7/33		1618	11/45		1627	6/50
	1611	4/49		1619	10/52		1628	4/47
	1612	3/46		1620		11/03	1629	3/46
	1613	7/47		1621	7/48		1630	1/46
	1614	10/48		1622			1631	4/53
	1615	5/36	10/03	1623	10/35		1632	11/45
	1616	12/50		1624	5/36		1633	7/42
				1625	9/33			

Plate 18   **D M Lee**
Siphon No 1591 and part of No 1567, both of Diagram O.5, and the former with a recently repaired end

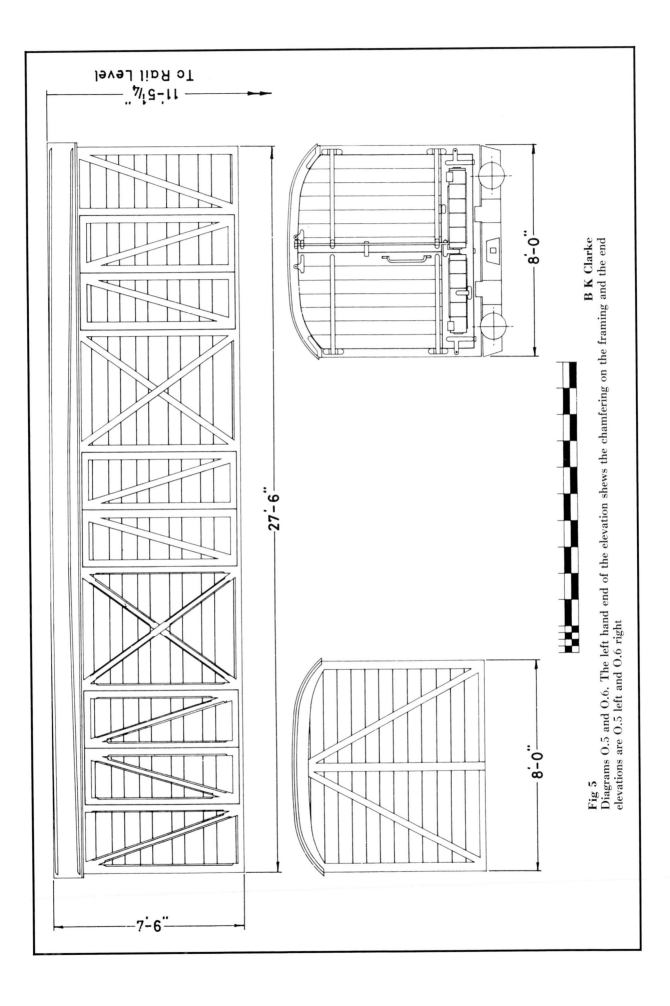

To Rail Level

11'-5¹⁄₄"

27'-6"

8'-0"

8'-0"

7'-6"

B K Clarke

Fig 5
Diagrams O.5 and O.6. The left hand end of the elevation shews the chamfering on the framing and the end elevations are O.5 left and O.6 right

LOT 1044

Dual fitted Vacuum and Westinghouse brakes

Built	No	Cond	Built	No	Cond	Built	No	Cond
12/03	1559	8/47	4/04	1576	5/54	6/04	1592	2/53
	1560	5/47		1577	3/45		1593	11/48
10/03	1561	12/52		1578	10/46		1594	11/46
	1562	3/48		1579		7/04	1595	4/49
	1563	7/59		1580	3/47		1596	3/46
	1564	6/47		1581	12/50		1597	1/47
1/04	1565	6/49		1582	10/47	8/04	1598	12/27
	1566	12/47	5/04	1583	12/48		1599	4/55
	1567	12/52		1584	12/47		1600	7/47
	1568	10/45		1585	10/47	10/04	1601	7/51
	1569	10/47		1586	6/53		1602	10/46
	1570	12/47		1587	8/47		1603	10/47
2/04	1571	5/47		1588	7/47		1604	3/47
	1572	8/47	6/04	1589	11/48		1605	5/47
	1573	12/47		1590	11/47	11/04	1606	6/49
4/04	1574	7/51		1591	1/56	10/04	1607	7/47
	1575	12/28					1608	5/47

Both the above Lots were described as Fish Vans until 1908 when they were listed as Milk Vans

NOTES

Nos 1561, 1576, 1586 and 1592 were sold on condemnation

No 1559 to Enparts Van No 198 in 4/44

No 1560 to Enparts Van No 199 in 2/44

No 1564 to Enparts Van No 200 in 7/44

No 1571 to Enparts Van No 201 in 7/44

No 1584 to Enparts Van No 202 in 7/44

No 1603 to Enparts Van No 203 in 7/44

No 1605 to Enparts Van No 204 in 7/44

No 1608 to Enparts Van No 205 in 7/44

No 1620 to Enparts Van No 206 in 7/44

No 1589 rebuilt with end doors as the prototype for Diagram O.6 under LOT 1082

The underframe of No 1579 was used for the tank wagon built on LOT 2112 in 4/49 as No B749500

No 1631 branded Return to Carmarthen (To carry milk churns only) in 12/49

No 1599 branded Lifton & Paddington in 9/50

The above Lots were on Passenger Diagram O.5 for which the Swindon ¼in Diagram Number was 22779 and later 24899

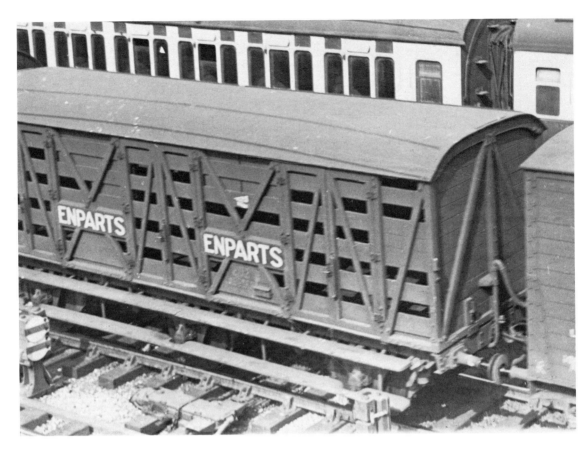

Plate 19   P Garland
A conversion to Enparts Van No 202 from Siphon No 1584

Diagram O.6

After a period of 26 years the last of the six wheel Siphons appeared in 1905. This Diagram on which there was only 11 Vans had all the previous standard dimensions with the difference that this Lot was provided with end doors. Below these doors was a full width drop flat and two wooden blocks on this laid on the buffer shanks when the flap was down to maintain a level loading platform with the floor.

LOT 1082

Built	No	Cond	Built	No	Cond	Built	No	Cond
1/05	1549	7/50	2/05	1552	3/52	2/05	1556	6/48
	1550	10/47	1/05	1553	10/42		1557	1/48
	1551	3/46		1554	1/50		1558	3/47
			2/05	1555	7/47			

Described as Milk Vans

NOTES
No 1552 sold on condemnation

34

The above Lot was on Passenger Diagram O.6 for which the Swindon ¼in Diagram Number was 29794

No 1589 of Lot 1044, after re-building, was also on this Diagram

Plate 20   **M Longridge**
A three quarter view of No 1552 of the only end door 6 wheel type showing the different pattern of doors from those on Siphon C and Siphon H

Plate 21   **From the Author's collection**
A mixed train leaving Penzance in the late XIXth Century with two ex-Broad Gauge fish trucks and one of the four wheel Siphons from the first two Lots of this design

PAINTING & LETTERING

The six wheel Siphons which came into service in the nineteenth century passed through all five of the lettering styles adopted by the railway from then until nationalisation. But one feature remained unchanged — the body colour was always coach brown for both sides and ends on a black underframe. Roofs were painted white but, with little washing and extensive use in traffic, the usual sight was nearer mud colour. Footboards were unpainted wood.

All vans built before 1904 carried lettering which leant a good deal on freight stock practice of the period. Indeed subsequent changes until 1934 was similarly based. The original style of lettering for the 2 door types comprised the letters G.W.R, with only two fullstops, in yellow on the top plank to the left of the left hand doors; these letters, like their freight stock counterparts were 6in deep, just fitting nicely within the depth of the plank. The number, in similar sized figures, was on the same level immediately to the right of the left hand doors. On three door examples the letters G.W.R. were on the top plank immediately to the left of the centre door with the number in the corresponding position to the right of this door. This pattern of lettering was similar to the practice of the earlier four wheel type where Company initials and number were either side of the central door on the top plank.

Plate 22   P Garland
No 1650 with the circular monogram where formerly the "G" of G W used to be

36

Plate 23
No 1628 with 1923 lettering

M Longridge

Load and tare weight were written in the Company's italic script and, in the two door versions were both crammed into the space on the bottom plank below the "G.W.R". On the three door types "Load" was below the letters and "Tare" below the number, in each case on the bottom plank.

Occasional vans were branded "For Fish Traffic Only" and this appeared in 6in block capital letters, one word to each plank, on four planks at the left hand side of the end starting with the plank at eaves level.

From 1904 when the new livery was adopted for freight stock these vans again followed that practice. With the open planked body there was no place where the new large letters could be put so the sides were modified by inserting a plank to fill the gap below the X-members of the side cross bracing; both of them for the two door types and the outside ones for those with three doors. One would have thought that a simple piece of sheeting would have been a cheaper solution to what was only a cosmetic problem. Once these parts of the side were made solid a "G" and "W" as large as would fit in were painted on, still in yellow.

This modification meant that for 3-door vans the load and tare writing had to be moved so the load moved to the extreme left of the bottom plank in the form "10 Tons" omitting the word "Load" while the tare weight moved to the extreme right hand of the same plank and was written in full *e.g.* "Tare 10.11.2." The Railway did nothing by halves and the number was also moved to the third plank up the side, above the "W" to the right of the centre of the X-bracing.

37

Plate 24   M South
Another 1923 lettering example on Siphon No 1565 fitted with Westinghouse brake

At this time legends appeared on the solebar in white paint. The overall length over buffers and the overall width over projections were painted below the "G" in the form $\frac{31\cdot5}{8\cdot9}$. Dual fitted vans had "WESTINGHOUSE BRAKE" written in two lines of blocks in a similar position at the right hand end of the solebar. For a short time, too, the vehicle number was carried on the fourth plank up the ends on the left hand side and the tare weight, in round tons, was painted four planks higher up.

There were no changes from this style until 1934 when the "shirt-button" monogram came into use all over the railway. This time the Siphons took their cue from passenger stock livery and adopted the Monogram. This took the place of the previous large "G" and the "W" was, of course, obliterated but the number was moved to this space on the bottom plank.

By 1938 when the use of the monogram on rolling stock was abandoned there were about 275 6 wheel Siphons still in traffic though, doubtless, many of these were already earmarked for condemnation. The war coming shortly gave these a new lease of life but it is doubtful if many were completely repainted before they were withdrawn. Many photographs have been seen with vestiges of an old monogram still visible but none with any later style of livery. There are many photographs of Siphons where the only lettering visible is the number and many more cases where even that cannot be distinguished.

Those vans converted to carry engine parts had boards with the name "ENPARTS" in large blocks on the middle of the sides with the new Departmental series number at the left hand end bottom plank. The code name "SIPHON" was never carried by any of these vans.

38

Plate 25　　　　　　　　　　　　　　　　　　　　　　　　**G E Houghton**
Blenheim with a representative selection of Siphons

Plate 26　　　　　　　　　　　　　　　　　　　　**From a postcard of Puxton**
Do not always believe what the branding on a Siphon says!

39

Diagram O.7

In 1907 a completely new design of milk van appeared from Swindon. It was the first of its class to be carried on bogies and, although only 40ft long, it appeared a massive vehicle. It continued the experiment started with Diagram O.6 in having end doors but broke new ground entirely by using louvre ventilators in place of the old open plank construction. The width was still 8ft but the body height was increased to 7ft 9in and all the class were dual vacuum and Westinghouse brake fitted. All this was obviously done to make the vans more versatile although they are described in the Lot List and on the Diagrams as "Milk Vans".

Both doors, of which there were four a side instead of the old maximum of three, were half boarded to waist level and surmounted by deep louvres. The end doors were similar to those on the O.6 Diagram with hinged portions above a narrow drop flat and the roof shape was the now standard 3-centre style. There was still the heavy outside framing below the waist level. Upper footboards at solebar level extended the whole length of the vehicle as did the lower steps but the central portion was later removed leaving the lower steps only on the bogies while the handle for the either side hand brake was now positioned centrally. They were gas lit and the by-pass cock handle for turning the lights low between stops was almost central on the van and about half way up the side and it could be reached through a hole in the door which was appropriately labelled. Steam pipes were fitted and the word "STEAM" in white block letters was written towards the right hand end of the solebar.

The class started life with 9ft wheelbase volute spring bogies but many were changed to the 9ft American type and some to 7ft heavy bogies. The massive appearance did not belie the capacity which was 18 tons and they had an average tare weight of about 22 tons. What bogie changes there were are listed in the table and the illustrations shew the detail of each of the different types of bogie. As only 6 were built it would seem this was to some extent an experimental design and this is borne out by the different style of later bogie milk vans.

The first vans were introduced after the 25in "G" and "W" lettering had come into use for freight stock and, like their 6 wheel predecessors, these vans followed freight lettering practice rather than coach practice. Like all Milk Vans on the GWR the body colour was brown with black at solebar and below and white roofs. All lettering in yellow and the first style had 25in letters actually upon the louvres centrally between the outer doors. This is a difficult painting job and it is not unexpected to find the letters removed to the body side below the louvres on the first re-painting;

Plate 27
Siphon F in the livery carried when first built but never afterwards perpetuated. This also shews the volute spring bogies

NUVB

41

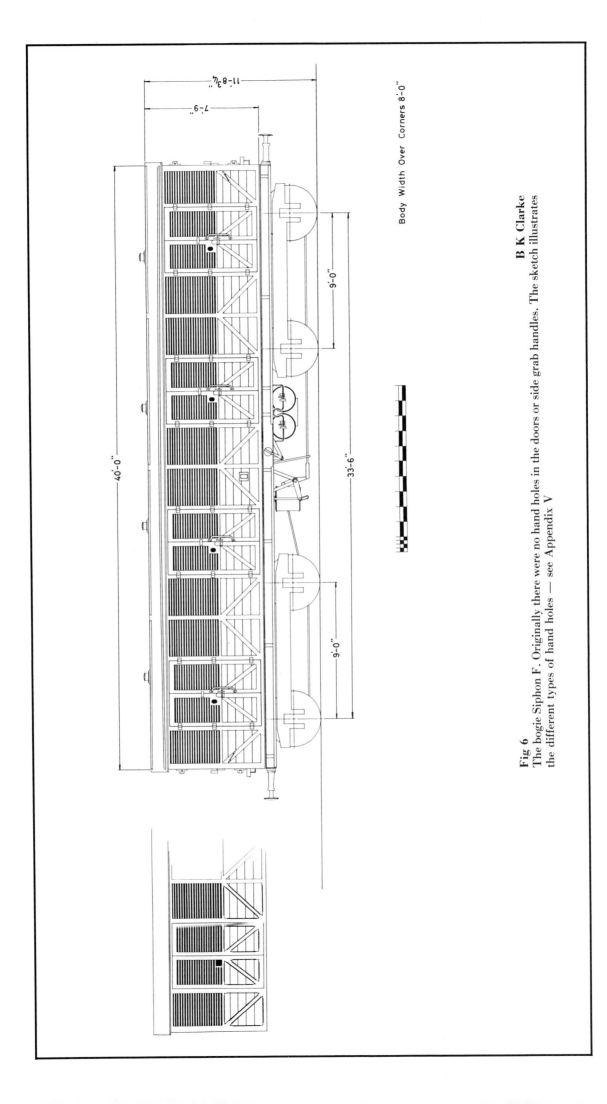

11'-8 3/4"

7'-9"

40'-0"

9'-0"

33'-6"

9'-0"

Body Width Over Corners 8'-0"

B K Clarke

Fig 6
The bogie Siphon F. Originally there were no hand holes in the doors or side grab handles. The sketch illustrates the different types of hand holes — see Appendix V

this probably did not happen until the 16in letter was introduced about 1923 when this size could be accommodated better than the larger ones among the outside framing.

The monogram was introduced, in common with all passenger stock, from 1934 taking the place on these vans of the former letter "G" and this change in principle from a freight based style of livery to a passenger based pattern (no true freight stock ever carried the monogram) seemed to place all milk vans into a livery limbo. When the monogram was discontinued on passenger carrying stock nothing appeared to be done to alter the painting of any of the Siphons. Indeed there are examples where the monogram can be clearly seen with the "W" prefix to serial numbers in BR days.

Until BR days the code name was not carried on the vans and all of them were on Passenger Diagram O.7.

LOT 1124

Built	No	Cond	Built	No	Cond	Built	No	Cond
8/06	1543	1/46	9/06	1545	8/53	9/06	1547	11/54
	1544	4/48		1546	3/56		1548	9/55

Plate 28   **P J Garland**
Siphon F No 1548 on 9ft American bogies. Note the gaps in the upper rainstrips

Plate 29   **M Longridge**
Shewing the brandings carried in BR days by vans used on the Harris sausage traffic. American bogies on No 1546

NOTES
No 1543 was branded "TO WORK BETWEEN MILFORD HAVEN AND PADDINGTON ONLY" in 9/28

Nos 1545 and 1547 were fitted with 7ft wheelbase heavy bogies in 9/29

Nos 1546 and 1548 were fitted with 9ft wheelbase "American" bogies but the dates are not recorded in the Swindon Van Register. It is believed the alteration was in 5/16.

No 1545 branded Calne & Newcastle in 8/50

No 1548 branded Calne & Newcastle in 9/50

This Lot was on Passenger Diagram O.7 for which the Swindon ¼in Diagram Number was 29792

Diagrams O.8 and O.9

At the same time as the bogie Siphon F was introduced a new short Siphon also made its appearance. It was apparent that the last of the six wheel milk vans had been seen and the new design was longer than these but had only four wheels. Several of the improvements that had been incorporated over the years that the six wheel version had been in production were perpetuated. Particularly the three doors each side and the provision of end doors. Also at this time there was a conscious decision to separate milk and fish traffic the latter being confined to purpose built fish vans and, although the Siphon vans continued to be called Milk Vans they were no doubt built and designed to be versatile enough to be used on various different traffics. Almost as a general utility van.

At 28ft 6in these vans were longer than previous small milk vans and the same length was adopted as a standard for both fish and fruit vans. Open planking for the sides was abandoned and the new vehicles were close boarded halfway up the sides with deep louvre ventilators above. Both upper and lower footboards were fitted from new and the vans were gaslit. They were equipped with both vacuum and Westinghouse brakes and either side handbrakes at the right hand end and had steam pipes to enable them to be marshalled anywhere within a passenger train.

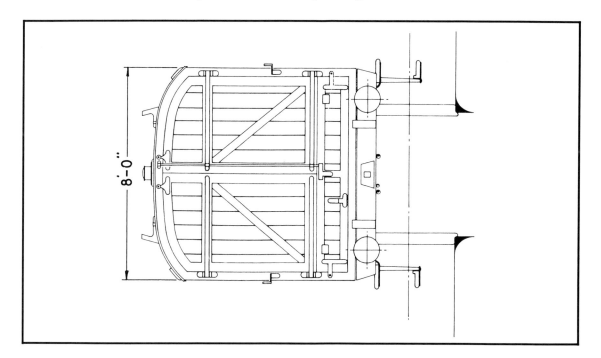

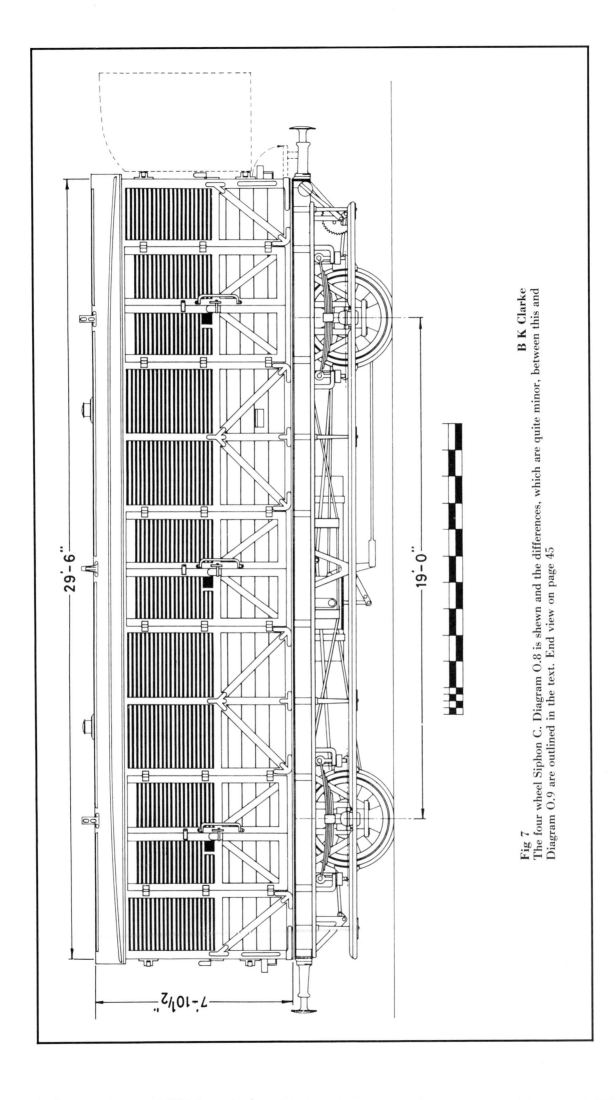

29′-6″

7′-10½″

19′-0″

Fig 7
The four wheel Siphon C. Diagram O.8 is shewn and the differences, which are quite minor, between this and Diagram O.9 are outlined in the text. End view on page 45

B K Clarke

NUVB

Plate 30
Siphon C No 1503 as built and the only example of end lettering on milk vans

The first examples were 8ft wide as in previous practice but it must have suddenly occurred to someone that contemporary passenger carrying stock was at least 9ft wide and that these vans would run in passenger trains so why should they not be wider. So from the middle of the second Lot the width was increased to 8ft 6in and this difference in width is the only distinguishing feature between the two Diagrams for these vans. Diagram O.8 is the narrow version and Diagram O.9 the wide one.

From the mid nineteen thirties these vans gravitated to the sausage traffic for C & J Harris of Calne and the table lists the brandings that are recorded. In BR days they stayed on this traffic and, in addition to the special headboards they carried large enamel plates emphasising and advertising the goods.

The painting and lettering closely followed the pattern just described under Siphon F but there were some differences. No attempt was made to put the letters on the louvres so, even in the 25in "GW" days the letters on the sides were smaller so that they might be fitted within the bracing but full size 25in "G" and "W" found sufficient room on the end doors. Also on the ends were the serial number and the words "Westinghouse Brake". The load was written on the bottom plank at the left hand end and the full tare in a similar position at the right hand end. The illustrations are clear enough on the main lettering. Overall length and width was in white blocks on the solebar as in the six wheel versions and the tare weight was also repeated to the left of these figures. "Westinghouse Brake" was written towards the right hand end of the solebar and, nearer to the middle, there was a gas pressure gauge.

Original photographs of the vans up to 9/20 indicate that the code name was not carried but shortly after other illustrations have the "Siphon C" on the bottom plank just to the right of the centre doors. Other evidence suggests that this practice was again discontinued but shortly before the 1939 war the name began to re-appear.

Plate 31   Source unknown
Siphon C No 1520 with 1934 monogram

48

Compared with the earlier Siphons there was a change of springing and suspension. A shorter spring on J-hangers was adopted and lower footboards were added in 1912 and remained until damaged when the supports were utilised to carry small steps.

Incandescent gas lighting, with roof pipes, was fitted from new to those on Lots 1133 and 1162 and to the remainder in 8/09.

LOT 1125

Built	No	Cond	Built	No	Cond	Built	No	Cond
11/06	1525	10/46	12/06	1531	10/33	1/07	1537	12/56
	1526	6/47		1532	1/47		1538	3/48
	1527	11/55		1533	11/49		1539	5/35
	1528	12/47		1534	1/47		1540	2/47
	1529	12/48		1535	9/56		1541	2/47
	1530	8/47		1536	2/49		1542	12/47

The above on Passenger Diagram O.8, Swindon ¼in Diagram 26980A

LOT 1133
part only

Built	No	Cond	Built	No	Cond
5/07	1515	11/49	5/07	1517	1/48
	1516	8/47		1518	11/56

The above were on Passenger Diagram O.8 for which the Swindon ¼in Diagram Number was 30453

LOT 1133
part only

Built	No	Cond	Built	No	Cond	Built	No	Cond
5/07	1519	2/47	12/07	1521		12/07	1523	6/56
12/07	1520	3/49		1522	3/48		1524	2/47

The above on Passenger Diagram O.9, Swindon ¼in Diagram 31515

LOT 1162

Built	No	Cond	Built	No	Cond	Built	No	Cond
3/09	1503	5/48	3/09	1507	10/48	5/09	1511	11/57
	1504	10/47		1508	5/49		1512	1/44
	1505	11/47		1509	1/58		1513	3/47
	1506	11/46		1510	12/48		1514	3/47

LOT 1183

Built	No	Cond	Built	No	Cond	Built	No	Cond
5/10	1482	4/49	7/10	1489	5/49	8/10	1495	5/49
	1483	3/49		1490	1/42		1496	10/57
	1484	12/47		1491	4/58	9/10	1497	1/48
	1485	11/56		1492	4/49		1498	10/47
	1486	10/55		1493	3/49		1499	12/48
	1487	4/49	8/10	1494	1/58		1500	6/58
	1488	10/47					1501	12/46

The above were on Passenger Diagram O.9, Swindon ¼in Diagram Number 35153

Plate 32   **M Longridge**
End door detail of a Siphon C

NOTES
Brandings — general
No 1527 "RETURN TO PENZANCE IMMEDIATELY" 1/19

No 1531 To work 8.55 p.m. Paddington to Llanelly & 8.30 a.m. Fishguard to Paddington 7/36

No 1534 6.50 p.m. Birmingham to Paddington)
        6.30 a.m. Paddington to Birmingham) written on solebar 12/17

No 1542 Return to Stourbridge — this van was fitted internally to carry pigeons

No 1519 6.50 p.m.   Birmingham to Paddington)
        6.30 a.m.   Paddington to Birmingham) written on solebar 12/17

No 1521 Return to Wolverhampton 9/37

No 1523 Yeovil & Crewe via Severn Tunnel 11/12

No 1511 Return to Stourbridge — this van was fitted internally to carry pigeons

No 1512 To work 8.50 p.m. Paddington to Llanelly
                8.30 a.m. Fishguard to Paddington 8/36

No 1514 Return to Wolverhampton 8/37

No 1498 "RETURN IMMEDIATELY TO PENZANCE" 1/25

No 1496 "RETURN IMMEDIATELY TO PENZANCE" 12/25

No 1487 "RETURN IMMEDIATELY TO PENZANCE" 2/25

No 1539 "RETURN IMMEDIATELY TO PENZANCE" 1/19

No 1536 Branded Return to Westbury between June & October 1918 when used for aeroplane traffic Westbury to Pewsey

Brandings — sausage traffic
All the early headboards for vans engaged in this traffic had "MESSRS C & J HARRIS SAUSAGE TRAFFIC" written before the stations served, which were:

No 1484 Calne & Sheffield 12/34

No 1486 Calne Stafford & Manchester 12/34

No 1491 this one merely branded "Return to Calne" 12/39

51

Plate 33   **D M Rouse**
The narrow Siphon C branded for Harris sausage traffic in early BR days. No W1527

No 1493 Calne Carlisle & Glasgow 9/32

No 1495 Calne Southampton & Portsmouth 12/34

No 1500 Calne Newport & Cardiff 12/34; return to Calne 1/38

No 1503 Calne & Bristol Temple Meads 3/29

No 1505 Calne Newport & Cardiff 12/34; return to Calne 11/35 & 11/38

No 1507 Calne & Crewe 12/34

No 1508 this one merely branded "Return to Calne" 12/33 to 1937

No 1509 Calne & Paddington 1/50

No 1517 this one merely branded "Return to Calne" 7/32 to 1937 & 12/39

No 1520 Calne Carlisle & Glasgow 9/32

No 1529 Calne Carlisle & Glasgow 12/32 to 12/38 and see below

No 1530 Calne & Reading 12/34

No 1532 Calne Carlisle & Glasgow 9/32

No 1537 Calne & Bristol Temple Meads 4/50

No 1538 this merely branded "Return to Calne" 12/34

No 1539 this merely branded "Return to Calne" 12/39

No 1540 Calne & Paddington 12/34

No 1541 Calne Carlisle & Glasgow 12/34

No 1492 Calne & Manchester 12/24

No 1496 Calne, Southampton & Portsmouth 12/34

No 1523 Calne & Reading 12/34

No 1524 Calne Newport & Cardiff 3/34

No 1529 Return to Penzance 1/15 and Return to Calne 12/39

The end doors were sealed by coach bolting the bottom door drop flap at the dates shewn.

1492   4/19   1538   11/35   1523   1/36   1532   1540   1541   2/36

1503   1507   1508   1495-7   1484   1486   1525   1529 all 3/36

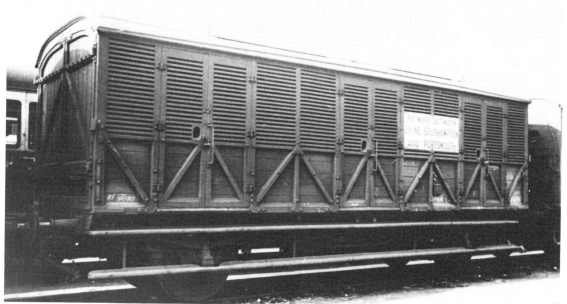

Plate 34   M Longridge
A Harris sausage van Siphon C No 1496 (Diagram O.9) with BR branding "Siphon C" in 1949

53

Plate 35

R H G Simpson

Part view of the prototype low roof bogie 50ft Siphon G

Diagram O.10

It may seem odd to commence an account of Siphon H with a low roofed one-off production but the diagram of this vehicle that has been inspected is labelled "Siphon H", no doubt because the vehicle had end doors. In later years this was altered to "Siphon G" and the probability is that the end doors were screwed up which would make it in most respects, apart from the provision of a gangway connection, similar to the Gs.

The Siphon C and Siphon F designs had obviously proved satisfactory and this one van was a prototype to determine whether an even larger version of the bogie milk van would be sensible.

There were several design changes incorporated. The low 3-centre roof was retained as were the end doors but the length was increased to 50ft and the greater width of 8ft 6in retained. The extra length meant that four double doors each side could now be accommodated but the most noticeable change in appearance was to the louvres. These were now roughly half the depth of the kind used on Siphon F and the close boarding of the sides beneath them was horizontal. When built it was equipped with 9ft wheelbase American bogies which were changed in November 1910 to 8ft coil spring types. In October 1931 these were again changed to 7ft wheelbase "heavy" bogies.

No evidence has come to light about the painting and lettering but there can be little doubt that this van was similar in all respects to the first batch of Siphon Gs. A distant view, taken in 1947, shews continuous footboards the whole length of the van where other 50ft milk vans had steps below the doors only. The print is too indistinct to shew any livery details.

Built with Westinghouse brake, through steam pipes and incandescent gas lighting with four lamps.

LOT 1164

Built	No	Cond	
10/08	1502	11/58	Diagram O.10 for which the Swindon ¼in diagram number was 37594

Diagram O.12

With this Diagram we come to the true Siphon H introduced in 1919. Although the outside framed Siphons of both Diagram G and Diagram H had a marked resemblance the batch about to be described were immediately recognisable from other types by the high arc roof reminiscent of the covered carriage trucks of the Python and Monster series. It is not exactly clear why this kind of van was thought necessary as the 3-centre roof bogie vans of Siphon G were the first result of the prototype bogie design described above.

The Siphon H was another 50ft van with four doors each side and with end doors. It is a tempting hypothesis to think that the batch was the result of having spare parts in stock. In 1910 the Company had built scenery vans of a very similar profile (the Monsters) but only two were completed and it could be that jigs and parts were on hand for others which were not constructed and that, in typical Swindon fashion, these bits and pieces were used up by building these milk vans. This, of course, is pure conjecture and it could also have been the case that the GWR required vans which were versatile enough to take high loads like the Monsters but which could be normally usefully employed carrying milk.

The width of these vans was again 8ft 6in but the body height was raised to 8ft 11¾in and they had angle iron trusses. Westinghouse brakes as well as vacuum were fitted with either side hand brakes with a centrally positioned lever; it is believed that

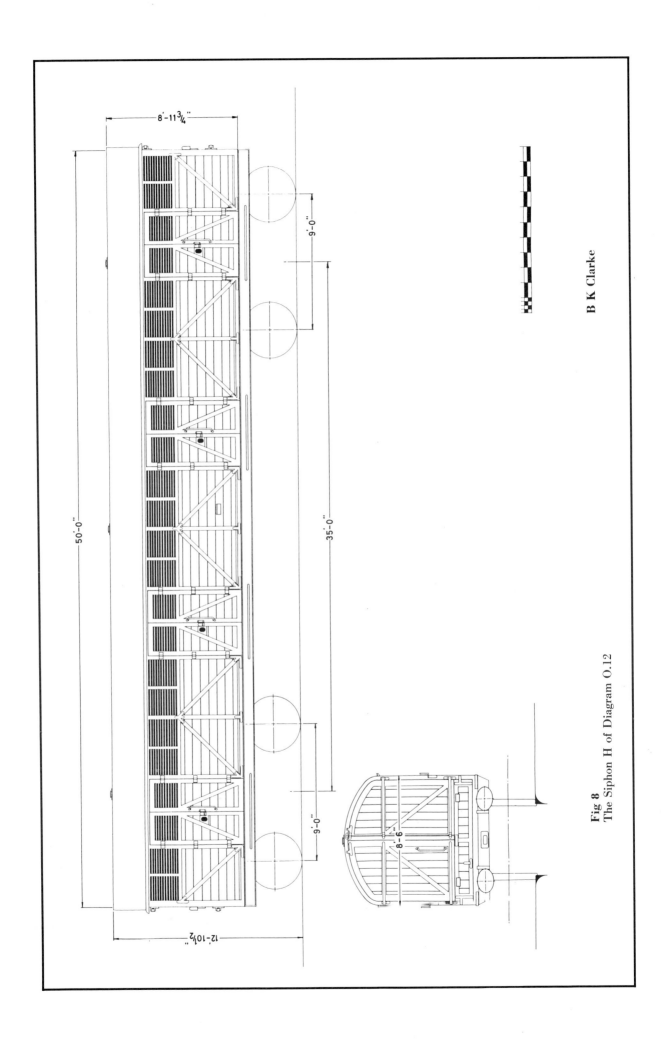

8'-11¾"

50'-0"

9'-0"

35'-0"

9'-0"

12'-10½"

8'-6"

B K Clarke

Fig 8
The Siphon H of Diagram O.12

Plate 36
Siphon H as built with the original style of double numbering

NUVB

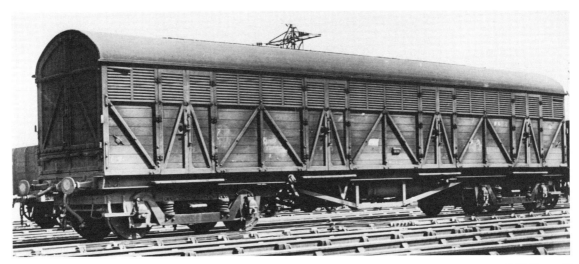

Plate 37   **J H Russell**
Siphon H, Diagram O.12, on 9ft American bogies. Identity unknown

at least some of these were later removed. The first seventeen vehicles were mounted on 9ft wheelbase coil spring bogies and the last three with the 9ft American pattern. There were changes and these are listed in the table.

Like all other milk vans the body colour was brown and the underframe black with white roofs. Lettering, in yellow, was the large "G" and "W" immediately to the left and right of the inner doors just below the louvres. The vans came into service during the 25in "GW" period so these letters were as large as could be painted within the outside bracing. When new the numbers were carried at both ends of the sides on the top plank but in the 16in "GW" style this was altered to one number each side, 3 planks up immediately to the left of the inner right hand door while the code name, Siphon H, in both styles was on the bottom plank just right of centre. Load at the extreme left hand end and tare at the right on bottom plank. With the introduction of the monogram the only change was its substitution for the earlier "G". In BR days the number appeared, with its "W" prefix, immediately to the left of the code name which remained unchanged and unmoved.

It is noted on the official Diagram that Nos 1422-30 had wood floors while Nos 1431-33 and 1435-41 had 'Sanit' floors — a waterproof compound. But, read literally, this has the intriguing inference that No 1434 had no floor at all!

LOT 1266

Built	No	Cond	Built	No	Cond	Built	No	Cond
2/19	1422	1/58	3/19	1429	12/56	6/19	1435	9/58
3/19	1423	1/56		1430	11/62		1436	7/58
4/19	1424	12/56		1431	9/60		1437	2/59
	1425	7/59	4/19	1432	10/59		1438	9/58
	1426	12/56		1433	11/62		1439	7/60
3/19	1427	8/59	6/19	1434	3/53	1/20	1440	1/59
	1428	1/59					1441	5/60

58

Plate 38   M Longridge
Siphon H No W1430 towards the end of its life mounted on American bogies

NOTES

No 1433 became Service vehicle No 079029 in 2/61

No 1441 became Service vehicle No 079061 in 6/60 and later (1966)
     sold to Messrs Woodhams

Bogie changes
No 1422 to 7ft wheelbase heavy 11/29

No 1424 to 9ft wheelbase "American" 8/30

No 1425 to 9ft wheelbase "American" 10/29

No 1426 to 9ft wheelbase "American"

No 1428 to 7ft wheelbase heavy 11/29 and later
     to 9ft wheelbase "American"

No 1430 to 9ft wheelbase "American"

No 1432 to 9ft wheelbase "American"; to 7ft wheelbase heavy 11/29

No 1434 to 9ft wheelbase "American" 5/30

No 1435 to 9ft wheelbase "American" 10/29

No 1438 to 7ft heavy 11/29

Brandings
No 1422 Neath to Sheffield 11/36
No 1432 Neath to Sheffield

SIPHON G

By 1913 the Company had determined what sort of Milk Van it needed to replace the obsolete ones in its fleet and the type that would prove to be useful and long-lived. Experience with the prototype 50ft van had obviously shewn this to be a versatile and useful design and between 1913 and 1955 365 vehicles of a basic family likeness were constructed.

The first change from the original one-off was the provision of gangway connections in place of end doors. Apparently what little advantage end doors shewed in traffic was greatly outweighed by the convenience of inter-coach connection. It meant, at least, that these vans could be marshalled at any position in a train without inconveniencing passengers.

All the vans built over this long period had a strong family resemblance but there were detail modifications and improvements as the years passed. The first batches were outside framed like the early Siphons to be followed by those with the bracing inside the body planking. The latter, too, changed from horizontal to vertical planking. Other noticeable differences concerned the ventilation. All these points are discussed in the notes Diagram by Diagram.

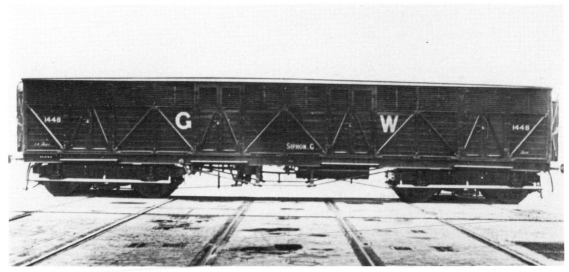

Plate 39   NUVB
Siphon G as built with the serial number each end and volute spring bogies with lower footboards

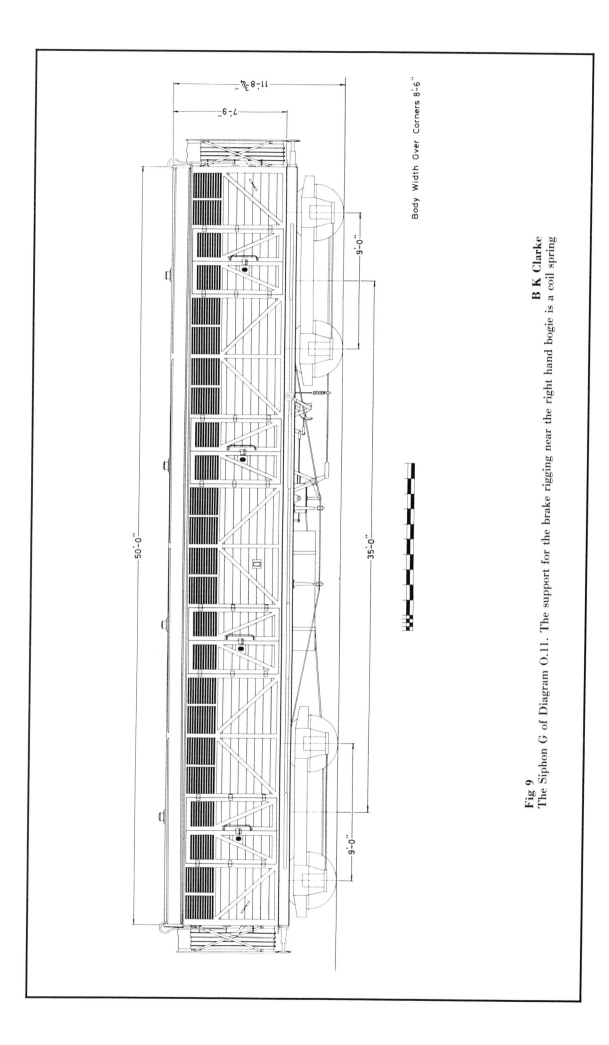

11'-8 3/4"

7'-9"

Body Width Over Corners 8'-6"

9'-0"

50'-0"

35'-0"

9'-0"

Fig 9
The Siphon G of Diagram O.11. The support for the brake rigging near the right hand bogie is a coil spring

B K Clarke

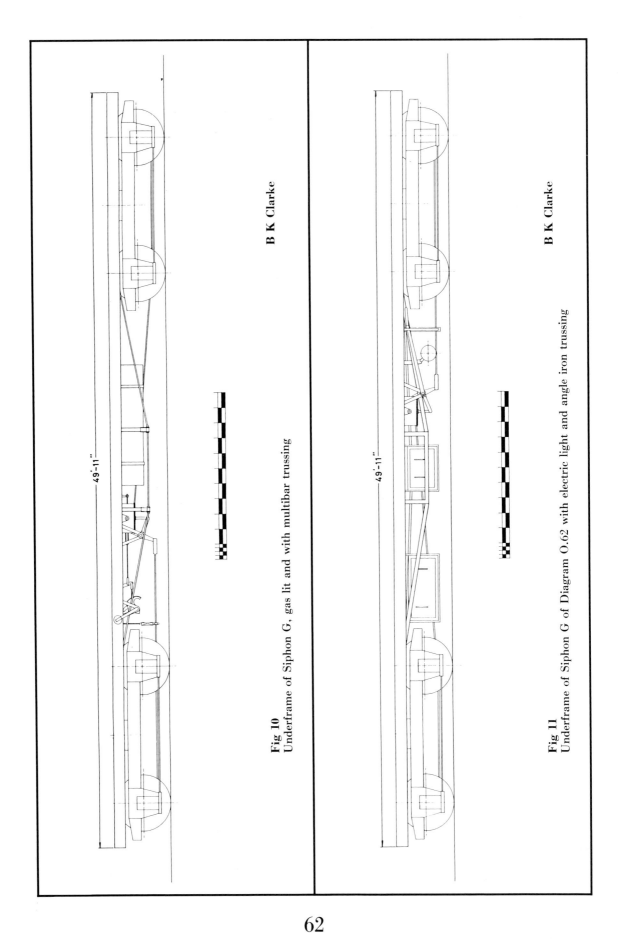

49'-11"

B K Clarke

Fig 10
Underframe of Siphon G, gas lit and with multibar trussing

49'-11"

B K Clarke

Fig 11
Underframe of Siphon G of Diagram O.62 with electric light and angle iron trussing

62

Diagram O.11

The first Siphon Gs followed the standards already used in being 50ft long and 8ft 6in wide with four double doors each side and the low 3-centre roof profile. Shallow louvre ventilators (compared with Siphon C and H) extended the whole length of the vehicle and scissors hung gangway connections were fitted. The sides below the louvres were of horizontal planking with the bracing outside and vacuum and either side hand brakes were standard. The handle for the latter was to the side of an inner door and between that and the bogie frame end. So on one side it was to the left of the van while from the other side to the right.

Lot 1211 had 10in channel solebars and flat bar trussing. The second Lot (Lot 1264) had similar solebars with multibar trussing consisting of round section bars attached to queen posts with the sloping parts of the trussing separate from the horizontal part. The remaining Lots had 9in solebars and fixed angle iron trusses. All except Lot 1347 were gas lit; the latter had electric lighting. They ran on 9ft wheelbase bogies but there were changes of type. Those that have been recorded are listed in the van histories but there may well have been many more as, with no change of wheelbase, there was no impelling reason to note a change of bogie nor to amend a Diagram.

Plate 40   NUVB
The second style of lettering of the Siphon G but still with volute spring bogies

LOT 1211

Built	No	Cond	Built	No	Cond	Built	No	Cond
1/13	1462	3/56	2/13	1469	11/56	3/13	1475	12/56
	1463	9/55		1470	12/56	4/13	1476	12/56
	1464	9/55	3/13	1471	4/55		1477	5/56
12/12	1465	11/56		1472	3/57		1478	7/57
	1466	10/55		1473	10/56		1479	4/55
	1467	9/57		1474	12/56		1480	12/55
2/13	1468	9/54				5/13	1481	2/55

NOTES

Bogie changes

No 1465 to 9ft wheelbase coil spring 6/19
       to 9ft wheelbase "American" 1/30
No 1468 to 9ft steel hornblock 6/19
No 1471 to 9ft steel hornblock 8/19
No 1473 to 9ft wheelbase coil spring 6/21
       to 9ft wheelbase "American" 12/28
No 1474 to 9ft wheelbase coil spring 8/19
       to 7ft wheelbase heavy 9/29
No 1478 to 7ft wheelbase heavy 9/29

LOT 1264

Built	No	Cond	Built	No	Cond	Built	No	Cond
6/16	1442	1/56	5/16	1449	11/56	4/16	1455	5/56
	1443	7/57	4/16	1450	5/56		1456	6/58
	1444	1/58	2/16	1451	12/55	12/15	1457	3/57
	1445	11/57	3/16	1452	1/59	1/16	1458	12/55
	1446	11/56		1453	3/57		1459	1/59
1/16	1447	9/55	4/16	1454	12/57	12/15	1460	3/57
	1448	1/59					1461	7/57

NOTES

Bogie changes

Nos 1442/54-56 originally with 9ft wheelbase "American"
Nos 1443-53/57-61 originally with 9ft wheelbase coil spring
No 1443 to 7ft wheelbase heavy 11/29
No 1447 to 9ft wheelbase "American" 6/25
No 1449 to 7ft wheelbase heavy 9/29
No 1452 to 7ft wheelbase heavy 10/29
No 1458 to 7ft wheelbase heavy 9/29
No 1459 to 9ft wheelbase "American" 8/19
No 1460 to 9ft wheelbase "American" 6/21

LOT 1316

Built	No	Cond	Built	No	Cond	Built	No	Cond
10/22	1345	12/60	12/22	1352	7/62	1/23	1358	7/58
	1346	11/60		1353	3/62		1359	1/61
	1347	6/59		1354	12/58		1360	7/60
	1348	7/61		1355	5/59		1361	1/59
	1349	11/61		1356	2/61		1362	10/58
11/22	1350	4/60	1/23	1357	7/62		1363	9/58
12/22	1351	4/59				5/23	1364	7/62

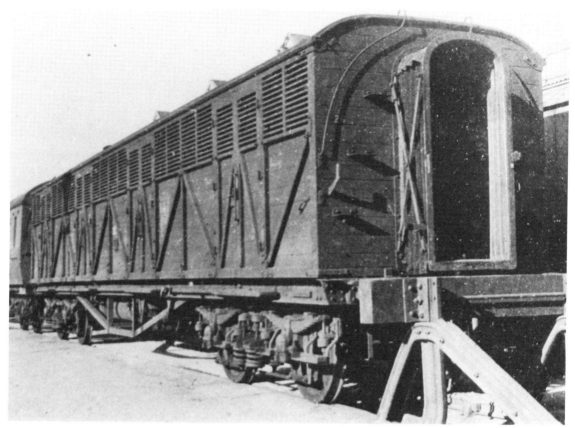

Plate 41   **P J Garland**

Siphon G No 1269 shewing the end steps and gangway, 7ft bogies and faint traces of 16″ G W livery

NOTES
Bogie changes

No 1357 to 9ft wheelbase steel hornblock 11/27; also Nos 1363/4

No 1359 to 8ft wheelbase coil spring when new

LOT 1347

Built	No	Cond	Built	No	Cond	Built	No	Cond
4/25	1290	12/62	6/25	1297	12/62	6/25	1303	9/58
	1291	12/62		1298	6/62		1304	6/62
	1292	6/62		1299	11/62		1305	9/60
	1293	8/61		1300	12/62		1306	8/62
	1294	1/60		1301	12/62		1307	8/62
	1295	11/61		1302	6/62		1308	4/62
	1296	9/62					1309	12/62

LOT 1368

Built	No	Cond	Built	No	Cond	Built	No	Cond
3/26	1271	9/62	4/26	1278	7/62	7/26	1284	12/62
	1272	8/58		1279	10/62		1285	12/58
	1273	12/62	6/26	1280	6/62		1286	4/62

	1274	12/58		1281	11/58		1287	12/62
	1275	3/59		1282	2/59		1288	12/61
4/26	1276	12/58	7/26	1283	1/46		1289	3/61
	1277	10/62						

Bogie change
No 1280 to 9ft wheelbase "American" 3/30

LOT 1378

Built	No	Cond	Built	No	Cond	Built	No	Cond
12/26	1240	3/62	6/27	1250	10/58	7/27	1259	1/62
	1241	1/62	7/27	1251	10/60		1260	12/62
1/27	1242	11/61		1252	12/60	9/27	1261	1/61
	1243	10/58		1253	8/60		1262	11/61
4/27	1244	11/62		1254	5/62		1263	1/60
	1245	10/61		1255	8/61		1264	12/62
5/27	1246	6/62		1256	10/58		1265	6/62
	1247	11/58		1257	2/59		1266	9/58
6/27	1248	10/60		1258	5/59		1267	9/58
	1249	11/61					1268	1/60
							1269	12/61

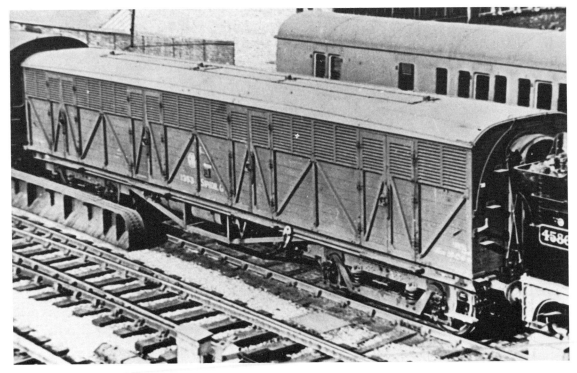

Plate 42   P Garland
A gas-lit Siphon G No 1353 with monogram lettering and shewing the piping arrangements on the roof

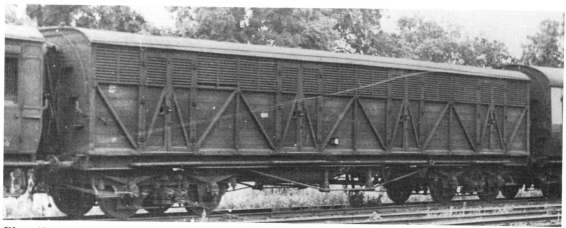

Plate 43
Siphon G, Diagram O.11, No W 1452, gas-lit and with 7ft bogies

P J Garland

NOTES
No 1261 became Service vehicle No 064716 5/61
No 1257 became Service vehicle No 079060 9/61; now on Severn Valley Railway
No 1267 became Service vehicle No 064721 8/61
No 1246)
No 1241) branded "TO WORK UP AND DOWN WEST OF ENGLAND TPO" 4/50

Bogies
Nos 1240-7/50-2 originally with 9ft wheelbase "American"
Nos 1248/9/53-69 originally with 7ft wheelbase heavy

The vans in this table of Lots originally ran on 9ft "American" bogies unless stated otherwise in the notes above.

Diagram O.22

The incidence of the First World War and the need to rehabilitate after it meant that little was done in the way of new milk van building and urgent needs were met by the adaptation of old saloons for milk traffic. The carriage works were busy on passenger carrying stock, particularly the refurbishment of ex-ambulance vehicles bought back from the War Department and apart from one Lot it was not until 1926 that further new bogie milk vans appeared.

The first order of the new design was just a one-off; almost as though it were a prototype to test some new ideas in construction. This vehicle, again 50ft long by 8ft 6in wide, differed from the previous Siphon Gs in having the side bracing inside giving an almost smooth exterior. It had the same general characteristics of narrow top side louvres and horizontal planking below. Gangway connectors were fitted, the van was electrically lit and it ran on 9ft wheelbase American bogies.

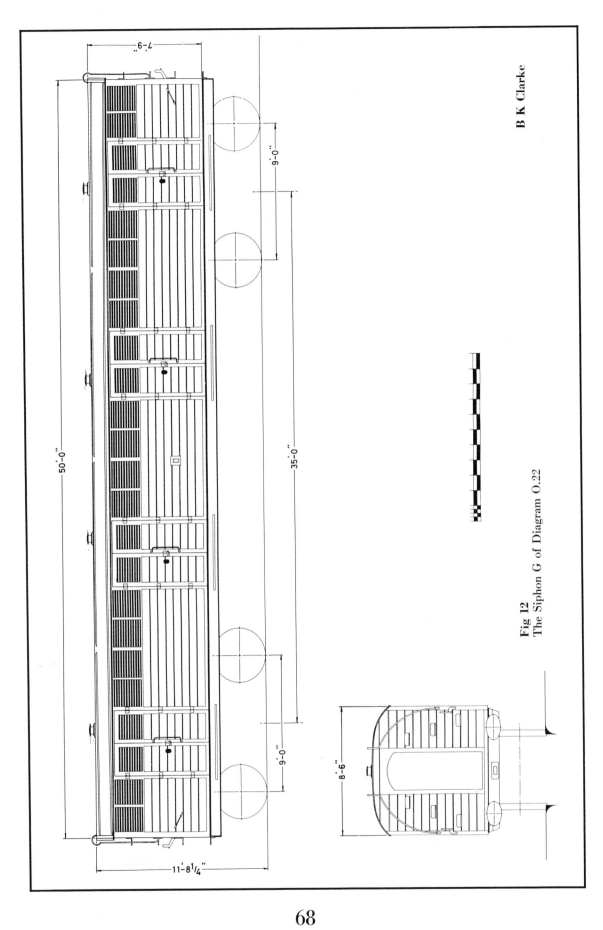

B K Clarke

Fig 12
The Siphon G of Diagram O.22

The design must have satisfied all concerned on the Railway and, in 1927, two more Lots were issued for a further 30 vans of similar type which were given 7ft wheelbase heavy bogies. Several of the last Lot, however, had the 9ft American type presumably because these were lying spare. This Diagram was electrically lit and had either side hand brakes with the handle mounted between the bogie and one of the inner pair of doors. The 3-centre style of roof profile had, of course, now become the standard.

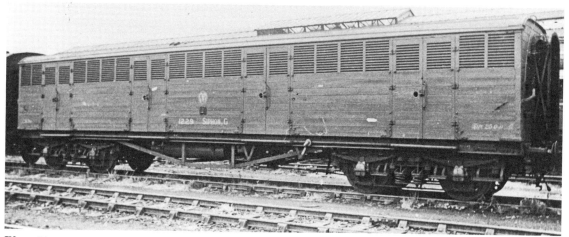

Plate 44
Inside framed Siphon G No 1229 in monogram livery

M Longridge

LOT 1370

Built	No	Cond	
8/26	1270	8/59	This was the "prototype" inside frame Siphon G fitted originally with 9ft wheelbase American bogies which were later changed to 7ft wheelbase heavy type.

LOT 1385

Built	No	Cond	Built	No	Cond	Built	No	Cond
11/27	1223	1/62	11/27	1228	3/62	2/28	1233	12/62
10/27	1224	12/62	12/27	1229	12/61	1/28	1234	12/62
11/27	1225	4/62		1230	1/62		1235	5/59
	1226	8/62		1231	12/61	2/28	1236	8/62
	1227	11/61		1232	10/62	5/28	1237	6/61

NOTES
Bogie changes
No 1228 to 9ft wheelbase American bogies

Brandings
No 1232 Penzance & Nottingham LNE 8/46
No 1233 Weymouth traffic 8/32
No 1234 Penzance & Leeds via Crewe 1/28 to 1932; Return to Yatton 5/49
No 1236 Penzance & Leeds via Crewe 1/28 to 1932

LOT 1396

Built	No	Cond	Built	No	Cond	Built	No	Cond
10/28	1186	3/62	10/28	1191	3/59	12/28	1196	7/61
	1187	12/62	11/28	1192	2/61	11/28	1197	7/61
	1188	4/62		1193	6/61		1198	11/61
	1189	12/62		1194	11/60	12/28	1199	1/62
	1190	8/62		1195	11/61		1200	1/62

NOTES

Nos 1190 and 1191 built with 7ft wheelbase heavy bogies
All remainder built with 9ft American bogies no changes recorded

No 1199 converted to Steam Heating Instruction Van No ADW 150322 in 1/62; withdrawn by 1983

Brandings
No 1186 Paddington & Neyland 4/53

No 1188 Return to Yatton 5/50

No 1193 Return to Yatton 6/38

No 1194 Liverpool Lime St to Penzance via Severn Tunnel 2/33 Pigeon traffic 5/36

No 1198 Return to Yatton 6/40

Swindon ¼in Diagram No 81289

Plate 45   NUVB
Interior of Siphon G shewing the collapsible racking on Diagram O.22

Diagram O.33

It would appear this new breed of Siphon G was eminently suitable to all Divisions of the GWR for in 1929 a new Lot 1401 was raised for the construction of 50 more to run on 7ft wheelbase heavy bogies and the serial numbers 2751 to 2800 were allocated to this Lot. For some reason the order was cancelled perhaps due to the introduction of milk tanks about this time, and doubts making the Company wonder whether milk vans were still necessary. However, in the following year all doubts had been dispelled and another Lot of Siphon Gs was completed. It would appear that the versatility of these vehicles for the carriage of traffic other than milk carried the day and, although all future Lots were designated as "Milk Vans", the actual vans were used for all sorts of traffic.

There was little difference between this new Diagram and its predecessors and what there was appears to have been instituted on economic grounds. The most noticeable change was to vertical planking below the louvres (these shorter lengths probably being cheaper) but they also had second hand sets of Stones Electric lighting and some even had the bogies recently freed from the gangwayed articulated coaches which had been converted to ordinary carriage stock. Vans on this Diagram are also 8ft 8in wide compared with their predecessors 8ft 6in and they had the new style of gangway connector hung from brackets fixed just below the roof line; they had, too, round headed buffers on the square tapered bodies.

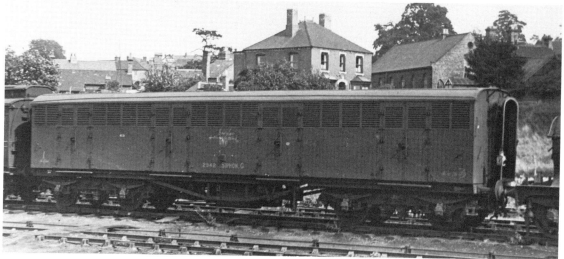

Plate 46   **P Garland**
No 2942 in monogram style lettering

LOT 1441

Built	No	Cond	Built	No	Cond	Built	No	Cond
7/30	2051	12/62	9/30	2058	12/62	10/30	2064	1/60
	2052	12/62		2059	11/62		2065	3/62
	2053	12/62		2060	11/62	11/30	2066	3/61

71

8/30	2054	12/62		2061	7/66			2067	12/62
	2055	3/65	10/30	2062	12/65			2068	11/56
	2056	3/62		2063	12/62			2069	12/62
	2057	12/62					12/30	2070	12/62

NOTES
Brandings
No 2052 Parcels Liverpool Lime St to Penzance via Severn Tunnel 2/33

No 2053 Return to Yatton 6/40

No 2055 Return to Yatton 5/50

No 2058 Return to Yatton 5/50

No 2060 To work between Paddington and Carmarthen 5/58

No 2064 Return to Yatton 5/39

No 2065 Return to Yatton 6/39

Plate 47   D M Lee
End view of Siphon G of Diagram O.33

Disposals

No 2055 to Enparts Van No ADW 150422 9/69; cond 6/81
No 2069 to Enparts Van No ADW 150428 11/69; cond 10/78
Nos 2061, 2062, 2064 and 2068 see under Diagram M 34
Nos 2063, 2065, 2067, 2069 and 2070 see under Diagram O 59

LOT 1578

Built	No	Cond	Built	No	Cond	Built	No	Cond
10/36	2751	1/63	10/36	2768		12/36	2784	11/62
	2752	12/62	11/36	2769	1/62		2785	1/68
	2753	6/80		2770	3/66		2786	1/63
	2754	3/73		2771	5/63		2787	12/62
	2755	1/63		2772	10/65		2788	5/61
	2756	12/62		2773	1/63		2789	7/66
	2757	7/66		2774	7/79		2790	
	2758	2/78		2775	10/57	1/37	2791	7/78
	2759	4/66		2776	2/66		2792	9/66
	2760	2/63		2777	12/62		2793	4/77
	2761	9/66	12/36	2778	10/65		2794	4/77
	2762	12/62		2779	3/62		2795	2/63
	2763	6/61		2780	1/63		2796	
	2764	2/67		2781	10/65	3/37	2797	11/56
	2765	12/78		2782	12/62	1/37	2798	1/62
	2766	1/65		2783	6/61	4/37	2799	7/78
	2767	12/66				5/37	2800	9/78

NOTES

Newspaper vans

The following were converted by BR to Newspaper Vans:

2758, 2765, 2774, 2791, 2793 and 2799
No 2796 preserved by GWS at Didcot

Disposals

No 2771 to Electricity Generator Coach for Exhibition Trains No TDB 975153
Nos 2752/4/7/8/9/61/3-5/8/70/4-6/8/81/3/9-93/8/99 see under Diagram M 34
Nos 2751/3/5-6/60/2/9/73/9/80/2/4-8/94-7/2800 see under Diagram O 59

Brandings

No 2753 Return to Yatton 5/38
No 2763 Return to Yatton 6/38
No 2766 Return to Yatton 6/38
No 2775 Return to Yatton 6/35
No 2776 Return to Yatton 5/50
No 2779 Return to Yatton 5/49
No 2785 For Postal Service 8/45

Bogies
This Lot was built with three different types of bogie. Some with standard new bogies and the remainder with bogies released from articulated passenger coaches which had been converted to run on two ordinary bogies. The allocation was as follows:

9ft pressed steel bogies: Nos 2751-71/3-7/81-6/9-91/3-4
8ft 6in single bolster bogies: Nos 2772/87-8/95-2800
8ft 6in double bolster bogies: Nos 2778-80/92

LOT 1651

Built	No	Cond	Built	No	Cond	Built	No	Cond
3/40	2917	5/78	3/40	2922	6/78	4/40	2927	7/79
	2918	1/69		2923	7/78		2928	1/72
	2919	7/79	4/40	2924	7/79	5/40	2929	4/79
	2920	6/79		2925	8/78		2930	11/78
	2921	7/79		2926	4/78		2931	

NOTES
All this Lot built with 9ft pressed steel bogies

Plate 48   NUVB
Interior of Siphon G of Diagram O.33

Disposals

No 2918 to Enparts Van No ADW 150427 11/69; cond 12/77
No 2923 to Enparts Van No ADB 975963 1980; cond 1/85
No 2924 to Enparts Van No ADB 975873 1979; cond 10/81
No 2925 to Enparts Van No ADB 975786 1978; cond 1/85
No 2930 see under Diagram M 34
Nos 2926/7/8 see under Diagram O 59

Brandings

No 2917 Down & Up West of England TPO 4/50
No 2918 Return to Yatton 6/49
No 2924 Penzance and Nottingham NE 8/46
No 2930 Cardiff and Birkenhead 7/48
No 2931 Return to Yatton 8/40

Plate 49   **GWR Magazine**
Siphon G No 2787 adapted for use in Penicillin Exhibition train

LOT 1664

Built	No	Cond	Built	No	Cond	Built	No	Cond
9/44	2937	5/78	12/44	2975	4/82	3/45	2985	4/77
	2938	1/85		2976	12/79		2986	2/72
10/44	2939	3/77		2977	10/78		2987	9/79
	2940	8/78		2978	8/78		2988	3/82
	2941	8/78	2/45	2979	6/78	4/45	2989	2/79
	2942	6/80		2980	5/78		2990	5/78
11/44	2943	11/78		2981	10/81		2991	4/72
	2944	5/78		2982	12/81		2992	8/78
12/44	2945	12/81		2983	3/82	5/45	2993	3/80
	2946	5/78		2984	6/78		2994	11/78

NOTES
Bogies

All this Lot were fitted with 9ft wheelbase heavy pressed steel bogies and no changes are recorded.

Disposals

No 2938 to Enparts Van No ADB 975774 11/78
No 2940 to Seat trimming material store No CDB 975840, 1979
No 2943 to Seat trimming material store No CDB 975841, 1979
No 2945 to Enparts Van No ADB 975788
No 2975 to Enparts Van No ADB 975777
No 2976 to Seat trimming store van No CDB 975842 10/79
No 2988 to Enparts Van No ADB 975789
No 2993 to Enparts Van No 975963, 1980
No 2994 to Seat trimming store No CDB 975843 10/79
Nos 2977 and 2978 see under Diagram M 34
Nos 2979-2984 see under Diagram O 59

Brandings

Nos 2937, 2945 and 2975 Return to Yatton, all in 5/50

General
No 2939 was selected for conversion to an automatic buffet car in 11/50 but the project was abandoned
Swindon ¼in Diagram Number 92209B
Nos 2940, 2943, 2976 and 2994 with their Departmental Numbers were still about in April 1985

Plate 50   M Longridge
Siphon G No 2057 of Diagram O.33 with monogram and BR "W" prefix to the number in 1949

76

CONVERSIONS

In 1938-9 the Government was concerned that if war was to break out the country would be immediately inflicted with saturation bombing with its attendant civilian casualties. To enable such a situation to be coped with it determined to have casualty evacuation trains ready to transport the injured to hospitals in safer zones.

The Great Western produced six of these trains, numbered 326 to 331, which comprised twelve vehicles each, nine of them altered Siphon Gs as ward cars, a third gangwayed brake at each end and a centre corridor third as accommodation for the staff. It is believed that the original intention was to replace the centre corridor third with restaurant cars when the latter could be suitably reconstructed but it is doubtful if this was ever done. However, later on in the war when these casualty trains were made into overseas ambulance trains the latter included adapted restaurant cars so the alterations probably went ahead but, with the lack of need for the casualty trains, the diners did not form part of the train make-up until the ambulance trains entered overseas service.

The alterations to the Siphon Gs were instantly noticeable from the outside as all the louvres were removed except for one in each pair of double doors. Apart from two windows one side and three the other all the louvres were sheeted over. Inside, accommodation was provided to carry 43 stretchers on brackets fitted to the side of the vans and steam heating pipes were run along the under side of the roof. The vans were identified by a yellow stripe on each corner but continued to carry their original

Plate 51   **GWR Magazine**
The conversion to casualty evacuation train coach of No 2067. Vehicle J of the train but still carrying the GWR insignia

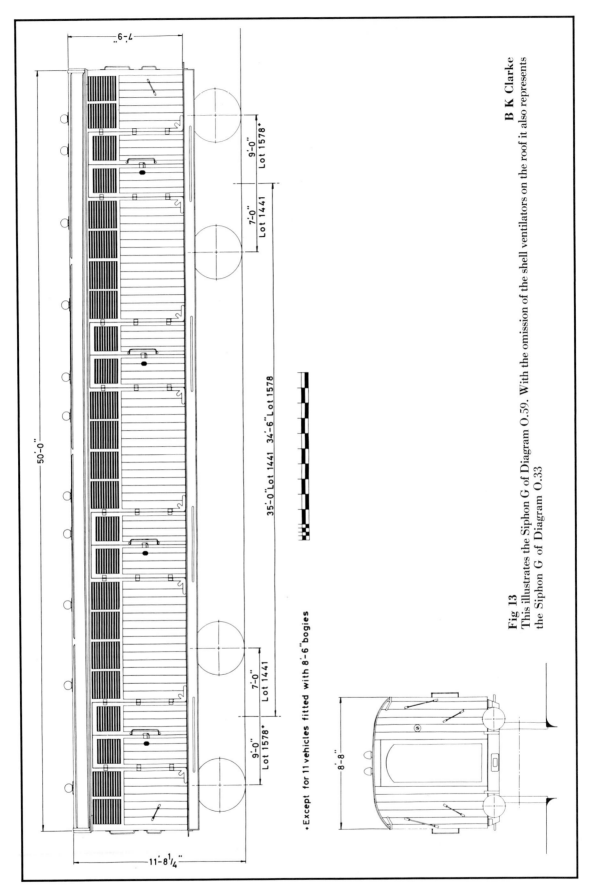

50'-0"

7'-9"

9'-0"
Lot 1578*

7'-0"
Lot 1441

35'-0" Lot 1441   34'-6" Lot 1578

7'-0"
Lot 1441

9'-0"
Lot 1578*

11'-8¼"

8'-8"

*Except for 11 vehicles fitted with 8'-6" bogies

B K Clarke

Fig 13
This illustrates the Siphon G of Diagram O.59. With the omission of the shell ventilators on the roof it also represents the Siphon G of Diagram O.33

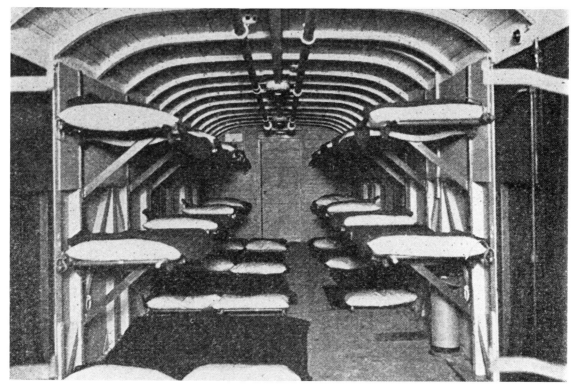

Plate 52
Interior of coach of casualty evacuation train

GWR Magazine

numbers. The brake thirds, of Diagram D 104, were divided between sanitation requirements and two tanks to hold hot and cold water together with a stove for cooking.

The alterations were completed in July and August 1939 and the Siphon Gs so altered were Nos 2061-3/4/5-70/2751/2/4-2800. The brake thirds completed at the same time were Nos 5133/5/6-9/5231/3/4/6/8/9/42 and the centre corridor coaches, Diagram C 68, Nos 4563/4/7-70.

By 1943 when the need for casualty trains had vanished the Siphon Gs were assimilated into ambulance trains for overseas which consisted of 14 vehicles each including the casualty conversions. The formations and constitution of these trains is outlined in Appendix III.

When these vans were returned from ambulance service two different approaches were made to their rehabilitation for normal traffic. These two types were on Diagrams M 34 and O 59.

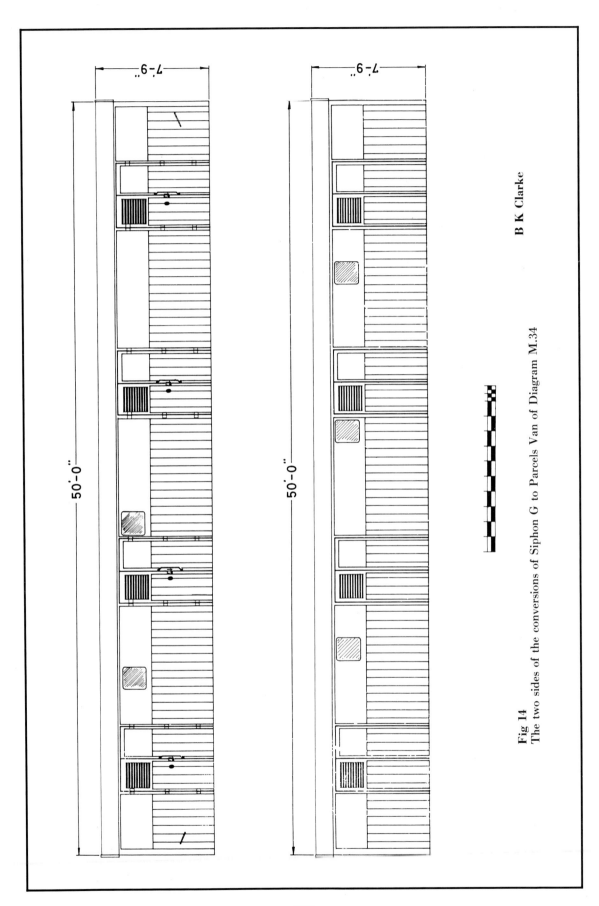

Fig 14
The two sides of the conversions of Siphon G to Parcels Van of Diagram M.34

B K Clarke

80

Diagram O.59

When the Siphon Gs were returned to the Railway after ending their use as ambulance vehicles conversion was basically to a milk van similar in appearance to their original state. The louvre ventilators were all replaced but the shell ventilators added on the roofs were not taken off nor apparently were the steam heating pipes. Indeed there is so little difference between Diagram O.59 and Diagram O.33 that the tracing for the latter, with the addition of shell ventilators, was used for the new Diagram. The basic difference in dimensions is an increase in overall height from rail level of $4\frac{3}{4}$ in.

Rebuilt to this Diagram
ex-LOT 1441
Nos 2063/5-7/9/70
ex-LOT 1578
Nos 2751/3/5-6/60/2/9/73/9/80/2/4-8/94-7/2800
ex-LOT 1651
Nos 2926/7/8
ex-LOT 1664
Nos 2979/80/1/2/3/4

Disposals
No 2065 to Enparts Van No ADW 150426 11/69; cond 7/81
No 2769 to Mobile Careers Centre No TDW 150327 4/62; cond 10/74
No 2981 to Enparts Van No ADB 975794; cond 10/81
No 2982 to Enparts Van No ADB 975790; cond 12/81
No 2983 to Enparts Van No u/k; preserved by the Gloucester and Warwick Railway
       after condemnation in 3/82

General
It is possible that, taking into account the dates into traffic, Nos 2979 to 2984 were never ambulance vehicles but built as Diagram O.59 Siphon Gs

Swindon $\frac{1}{4}$ in Diagram Number 128609

Diagram M.34

The remainder of the vans which came back from war service received a more radical alteration. For the first time for vehicles of this type the designation was changed to "Parcels Van" from "Milk Van" and the exterior was unaltered from the modification effected for ambulance use. Shell ventilators and steam heating apparatus was left on the vans and, like their companions on Diagram O.59, they resumed their previous numbers.

Plate 55 (overleaf lower)
No 2070 with 9ft wheelbase American bogies

M Longridge

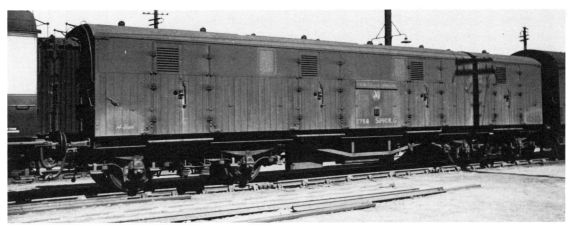

Plate 53   **M Longridge**
No 2758 converted to parcels van after ambulance train use

Plate 54   **M Longridge**
No 2796 fitted with 8ft 6in wheelbase bogies taken from converted articulated stock

Plate 56   J H Lewis
The lettering of bogie Siphon G (ex No 2981) converted to Enparts Van No ADB 975794

Rebuilt to this Diagram
ex-LOT 1441
Nos 2061/2/4/8
ex-LOT 1578
Nos 2752/4/7/8/9/61/3/4/5/8/70/4/5/6/8/81/3/9/90/1/2/3/8/9
ex-LOT 1651
No 2930
ex-LOT 1664
Nos 2977/8

Plate 57   **M Longridge**
Diagram M.34, Siphon G, No 2930 in the last form of GWR livery and branded for Plymouth traffic

Newspaper Vans
Nos 2930 and 2978 were converted by BR to Newspaper Vans

Plate 58   **M Longridge**
No W2062 branded for use as Newspaper Van — "To work on the 12.5 am Paddington News"

Plate 59   **J H Lewis**
Siphon G No W2960 pf Diagram O.59 clearly shewing the shell ventilators

84

Disposals

No 2759 to Seat Trimming Material Store No CDB 975838, 1979

No 2790 to Exhibition Train Generator Van No TDW 150027, 1957

No 2793 to Enparts Van No ADB 975656; then to internal use as No 041552 in
    4/81

No 2930 to Seat Trimming Material Store No CDB 975839, 1979

No 2978 became a stores van at Laira in 11/78

No 2775 to Stores van No TDW 150028

Swindon ¼in Diagram Number 128585

Nos 2759, 2790, 2793 and 2930 with their Departmental Number were still about
  in April 1985

Diagram O.62

With this Diagram we come to the end of the saga of the Siphon G. It was a design which had lasted unchanged in its basic details from its inception and had obviously proved its worth not only for milk traffic. Surprisingly enough the last pattern, produced by BR between 1951 and 1955, still referred to itself on the official diagram as a milk van.

The appearance of the last batches was little different from the predecessors adopting the standard three centre roof profile, the gangway connectors and the narrow band of louvre ventilators just below roof level. But there were eight extra louvre ventilators spaced along the sides immediately above solebar level and these ventilators had sliding shutters which moved vertically so that the openings may be blanked off.

Angle iron trussing and 9ft wheelbase heavy steel bogies were standard but there were changes to bogie types and 9ft American have been observed.

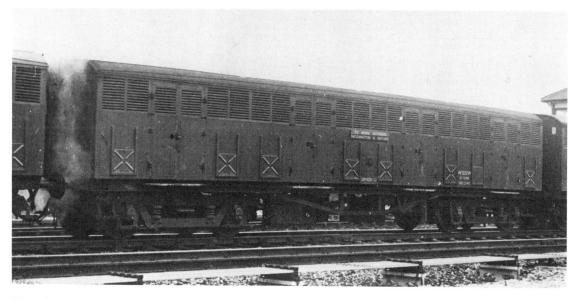

Plate 60　　　　　　　　　　　　　　　　　　　　　　　　　　**D J Hyde**
W1332W branded "To work between Paddington and Oxford"

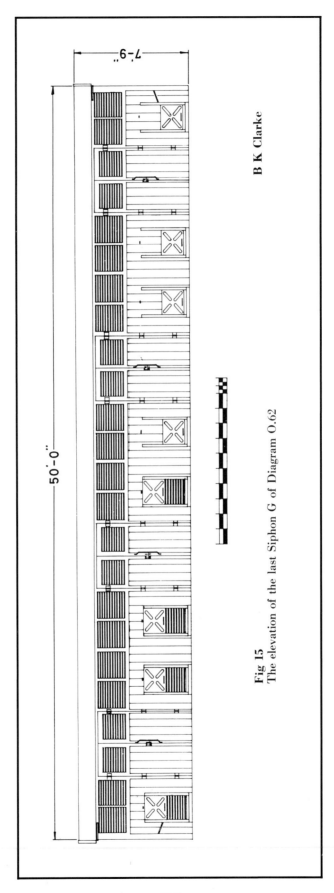

7'-9"

50'-0"

B K Clarke

Fig 15
The elevation of the last Siphon G of Diagram O.62

LOT 1721

Built	No	Cond	Built	No	Cond	Built	No	Cond
10/50	1310	8/78	11/50	1320	7/79	12/50	1330	6/73
12/50	1311	10/78		1321	12/78		1331	10/78
10/50	1312	8/81		1322	5/78		1332	1/83
	1313	8/81		1323	8/78		1333	11/56
	1314	6/78		1324	12/78		1334	10/59
	1315	7/71		1325	6/81		1335	11/82
11/50	1316	2/79	12/50	1326	12/78		1336	
	1317	2/79		1327	3/79		1337	4/79
	1318	7/78		1328	9/82		1338	8/78
	1319			1329	5/79		1339	8/78

LOT 1751

Built	No	Cond	Built	No	Cond	Built	No	Cond
4/51	1001	5/78	5/51	1011	3/79	9/51	1021	1/80
	1002	7/78		1012	11/79		1022	5/78
	1003	8/80	6/51	1013	5/80		1023	8/80
5/51	1004	4/79		1014	6/78		1024	1/83
	1005	2/79	8/51	1015	5/78		1025	11/78
	1006	7/78		1016	3/79	10/51	1026	1/83
	1007	11/82		1017	11/82		1027	11/63
	1008	11/79		1018	2/79	11/51	1028	11/78
	1009	9/79	9/51	1019	1/83		1029	11/78
	1010	8/80		1020	6/78	12/51	1030	2/79

LOT 1768

Built	No	Cond	Built	No	Cond	Built	No	Cond
4/55	1031	8/82	7/55	1038	3/79	7/55	1044	5/79
	1032	5/78	6/55	1039	7/78	8/55	1045	5/78
	1033	6/79		1040	6/78		1046	4/79
5/55	1034	1/83	7/55	1041	7/72	9/55	1047	1/83
	1035	11/82		1042	2/79		1048	10/82
	1036	7/79		1043	11/78		1049	7/78
6/55	1037	7/78				10/55	1050	11/79

NOTES
No 1332 changed to 9ft wheelbase American bogies early in life.
Swindon¼in Diagram Number 128197A

Plate 61   A E West
W1036 branded "To work only on Down and Up West of England TPO"

Plate 62   P W Bartlett
W1326 with latest BR logo and with all louvres except those at extreme ends boarded-up on conversion to Newspaper Van. Swindon May 1979

Disposals

The following were re-classified and branded for carrying newspapers:

Lot 1721 Nos 1312/20/4-9/32/5/7
Lot 1751 Nos 1003-5/7/10-1/3/6-9/23-4/6/30
Lot 1768 Nos 1031/4-5/8/44/6-8

And there were the following uses as Departmental stock:

No 1310 to Enparts Van No ADB 975785, 1978;	cond 3/85
No 1311 to Enparts Van No ADB 975791	cond 10/81
No 1314 to Enparts Van No ADB 975781	cond 10/81
No 1315 to Electric Generator for Exhibition Train No TDB 975152	cond 5/77
No 1318 to Enparts Van No ADB 975787	cond 10/81
No 1321 to Seat trimming material store No CDB 975836, 1979	
No 1327 to Seat trimming material store No CDB 975857, 1979	
No 1337 to Enparts Van No ADB 975869, 1979	
No 1338 to Enparts Van No ADB 975963, 1979	cond 10/81
No 1339 to Seat trimming material store No CDB 975837, 1979	
No 1004 to CCE stores van No ADB 975852	cond 3/82
No 1005 to Enparts Van No ADB 975868	cond 3/82
No 1006 to Enparts Van No ADB 975784, 1978 and to internal use as No 061046	
No 1008 to Enparts Van No ADB 975879	cond /82
No 1011 to Seat trimming material store No CDB 975856, 1979	
No 1014 to Enparts Van No ADB 975779, 1978	cond 1/85
No 1018 to CCE stores van No ADB 975853	cond 4/82
No 1020 to Enparts Van No ADB 975782	cond 10/81
No 1021 to Enparts Van No ADB 975935	cond 12/81
No 1022 to Enparts Van No ADB 975775	cond 12/82
No 1025 to Seat trimming material store No CDB 975832, 1979	
No 1028 to Enparts Van No ADB 975831	
No 1029 to Seat trimming material store No CDB 975833, 1979	
No 1032 to Enparts Van No ADB 975778	
No 1033 to Enparts Van No ADB 975871, 1979	
No 1036 to Enparts Van No ADB 975872, 1979	
No 1038 to Seat trimming material store No CDB 975855, 1979	
No 1042 to Seat trimming material store No CDB 975854, 1979	
No 1043 to Seat trimming material store No CDB 975834, 1979	
No 1045 to Enparts Van No ADB 975780	cond 4/82
No 1050 to Enparts Van No ADB 975880, 1979	cond 1/85

In all the foregoing lists the full TOPS prefix of three letters is given to differentiate the Departmental users. Some of the vans may have carried only the two letters "DW" or "DB"

Nos 1321, 1327, 1339, 1006, 1011, 1025, 1029, 1033, 1036, 1038, 1042 and 1043 under their Departmental Numbers were still extant in April 1985

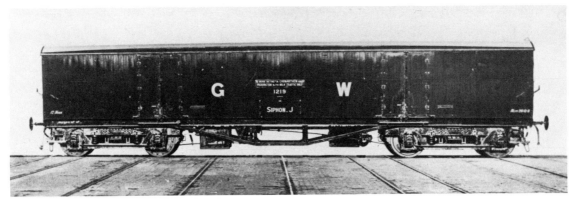

Plate 63
Siphon J as built with 9ft wheelbase bogies

NUVB

Diagrams O.31 and O.40

From the end of the development of the Siphon G as late as 1955 we must now go back to the 1930s to consider the only bogie Siphon type not so far discussed. This design differed from all other Siphon vans in that it did not have any means of ventilation from the outside and possessed perfectly smooth vertical planked sides and ends. There were no gangway connectors but the other attributes of the class such as the 3-centre roof and underframe details were similar.

The introduction of these vans brought the concept of insulation and cooling to the carriage of milk traffic. They were provided with ice boxes inside and the bodies were consequently insulated to ensure they stayed cool. There had already been some use of insulated and refrigerated MICA B vans for the carriage of milk and this was the logical step forward.

There were eight of the ice boxes on the sides, three quarters of the way up, while the roofs, sides and ends were double cased. They could accommodate 100-116 churns, four abreast across the body, and the Diagram is unique in that it shews this loading. Because of their specialist nature it was inevitable that their use was restricted to certain services and most of the vans carried a large board amidships with the details of its duty written on it in italic script.

Diagram O.31 is drawn to shew 7ft wheelbase heavy bogies but the original vans came out with 9ft wheelbase American bogies all of which were changed as shewn in the table. While they were carried on the longer wheelbase bogies their load was kept to 12T but, with the introduction of the 7ft type, this was raised to 15T. The later design on Diagram O.40 which reverted to a bogie of 9ft wheelbase was always designated to carry 12T.

The only difference between the two diagrams was the bogie wheelbase and hence the overall wheelbase but Diagram O.31 was also ½in higher.

Plate 64
Interior of Siphon J

NUVB

Diagram O.31

LOT 1409

Built	No	7ft bogie	Cond	Built	No	7ft bogie	Cond
2/30	1215	12/32	3/62	2/30	1219	12/31	4/62
	1216	12/31	12/62		1220	1/32	6/62
	1217	4/32	8/62		1221	12/31	9/61
	1218	12/31	11/61		1222	12/31	12/62

This batch was built with 9ft American bogies and these were changed as above

LOT 1463

Built	No	Cond	Built	No	Cond	Built	No	Cond
4/31	2024	5/62	6/31	2033	12/62	8/31	2042	12/62
	2025	1/69		2034	10/62	10/31	2043	12/62
	2026	11/64	7/31	2035	12/62		2044	7/62
5/31	2027	4/62		2036	5/62		2045	3/62
	2028	10/61		2037	9/62		2046	10/61
	2029	10/62		2038	7/62	11/31	2047	12/62
	2030	10/62	8/31	2039	12/62		2048	8/62
6/31	2031	12/62		2040	8/62		2049	9/62
	2032	3/62		2041	10/61		2050	10/62

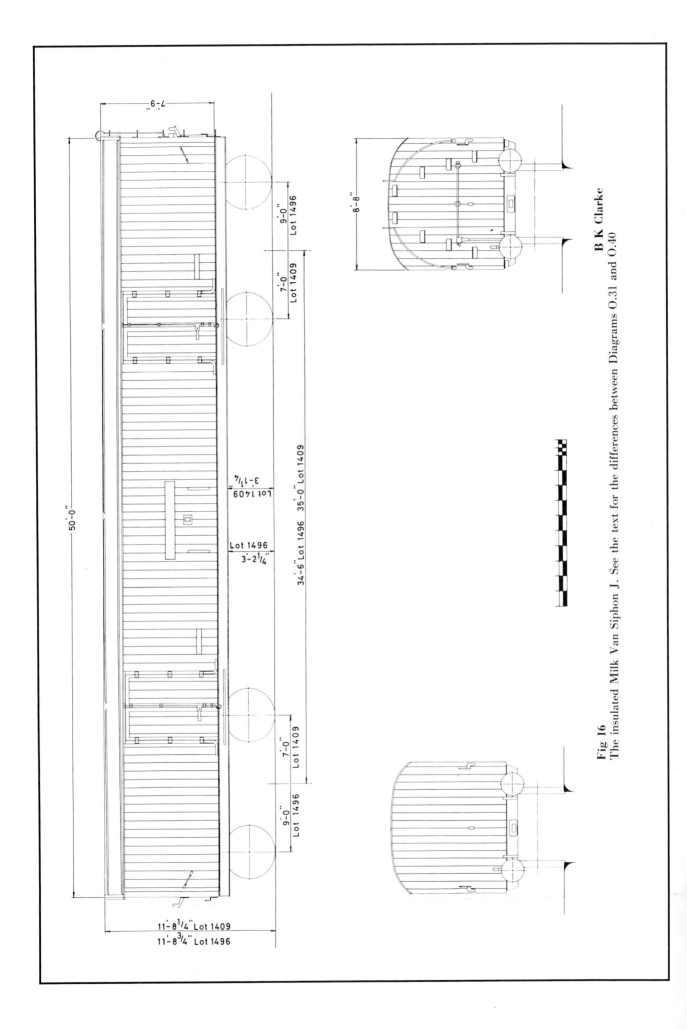

Fig 16
The insulated Milk Van Siphon J. See the text for the differences between Diagrams O.31 and O.40

B K Clarke

This batch built with 7ft wheelbase heavy bogies.
Both Lots had second hand Stones Electric lighting equipment

Diagram O.40

LOT 1496

Built	No	Cond	Built	No	Cond	Built	No	Cond
4/34	2518	10/61	4/34	2521	7/61	4/34	2525	5/62
	2519	5/62		2522	12/62		2526	12/62
	2520	12/62		2523	10/62		2527	12/62
				2524	8/62			

This batch built with 9ft wheelbase pressed steel bogies

Plate 65   L E Copeland
Siphon J No 2046, with 7ft wheelbase bogies, in traffic shortly after building

Plate 66   M Longridge
Siphon J, No 2049, Diagram O.31. The branding is "Return to Sparkford" despite what is said in the text

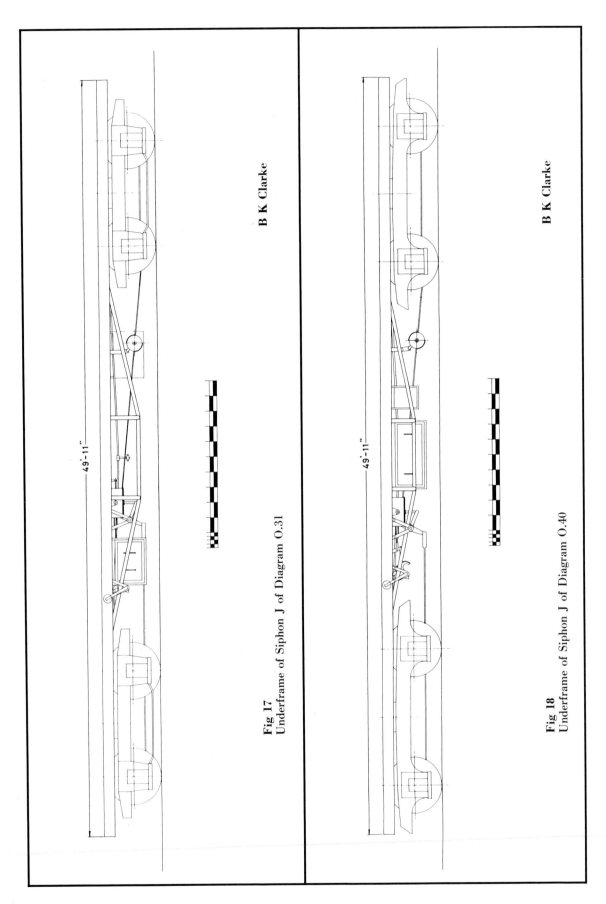

49'-11"

B K Clarke

Fig 17
Underframe of Siphon J of Diagram O.31

49'-11"

B K Clarke

Fig 18
Underframe of Siphon J of Diagram O.40

Brandings

The boards fitted to the sides of these vans to carry the details of traffic worked had the wording which took the form: "To work between . . . and . . . with milk traffic only" in italic script with the dots above replaced by the names of the stations or depots served. The table below shews these places with the dates from which the legends were borne. Where no dates are given it can be assumed that the board dates from the introduction into traffic. No specific alterations are shewn but the date is that from which an individual serial carried that board.

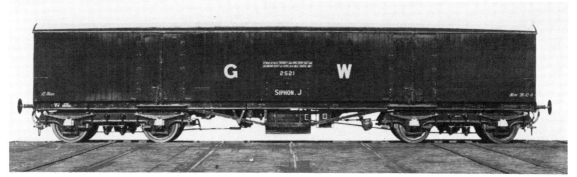

Plate 67   NUVB
No 2521 as built with 7ft wheelbase bogies

Plate 68   M Longridge
End view of a Siphon J

Places	Serial Nos		
Sparkford and Paddington	2025/6/8/9	from	4/31
Sparkford and South Lambeth	2027/30	from	4/31
	2049	from	1/34
Carmarthen and Paddington	2031/5/6/7		
	2044	from	12/32
Ilminster and Paddington	2032/3/4/26	from	4/31
	2050	from	1/33
Lodge Hill and Paddington	2038/9/40		
Baschurch and Paddington	2041/2		
	2025	from	5/38
Salisbury & Kensington Addison Rd	2043/4		
Somerton and Paddington	2045/6		
Badminton and Paddington	2049/50		
Moreton-in-Marsh and Paddington	2043	from	12/32
	2047/8	from	5/35
Langport West and Paddington	2045	from	12/32
	2046	from	4/35
Thorney & Kingsbury Halt & Gillingham (Kent) via Yeovil	2521/2/3	from	4/35

There was also other types of wording which did not follow the above pattern:

RETURN TO SPARKFORD	2026/8/9/30	from	10/31
RETURN TO CARDIFF	2038/9/40	from	3/37
RETURN TO CARMARTHEN MILK CHURNS ONLY	2049/50	from	12/40
RETURN TO MORETON-IN-MARSH	2524/5/6	from	1/35
FOR MILK TRAFFIC ONLY RETURN TO MARTOCK GWR	2524	from	10/37
RETURN TO YATTON	1220	from	6/40

Boards were removed as follows:

2043 in 12/37; 2045/6 in 10/37; 2047/8 in 12/37; 2023 in 10/38; 2025 in 3/35; 2026 in 12/37; 2523 in 9/37; 2525 in 3/36; 2526 in 3/37;

Other alterations

Nos 2046 and 2523 were fitted, in 9/37, with 20 hooks in the roof and transferred to Fishguard for meat traffic

Diagram O.31 was on Swindon ¼in Diagram Number 87851A and O.40 on Number 102477

BOGIE SIPHON LIVERIES

Until 1934 all these vans bore a form of lettering that was analagous to the freight livery of the Railway (see "Great Western Way" by the author and published by HMRS for drawings and illustrations). According to the date of introduction of the van this would mean 25in letters "G" and "W" up to about 1923 when the size of the letters was reduced to 16in.

When the Siphon G and Siphon H were first painted they carried their serial numbers at both ends of the sides just below louvre level but this was a short-lived style. Numbers, once only, descended to the bottom plank centrally to the end of the Company's existence. In 1934 there was a change to the passenger style with the adoption of the "shirt button" monogram of the letters GWR. All the bogie Siphons carried their telegraph code names and all had brown bodies and ends with black underframes and white roofs. After the change of lettering style in 1934 there was no further alteration to the livery. All lettering in yellow paint.

From 1949 BR continued to rate the Siphons as passenger vehicles and to paint them accordingly. Initially they were plain crimson with yellow lettering but from mid-1956 the body colour changed to maroon.

In later BR days most of those that were appropriated for Newspaper traffic had the BR "crossover" logo and the word "Newspapers" in bold lettering to the left hand end of the side and the details of number, load and tare between the second and third vertical ventilators in from the right hand end. These vans were painted blue and TOPS coded NNV or NMV.

Plate 69   Source unknown
Siphon J of Diagram O.40, No W1221W in the last tyle of livery for this class of van

97

SIPHON BOGIES

Plate 70   M Longridge
The 9ft wheelbase bogie with volute springs which were later altered to coil springs

Plate 71   M Longridge
The 9ft wheelbase bogie with equalising beam; the "American" bogie

Plate 72   M Longridge
The 8ft 6in wheelbase bogie originally used under articulated passenger coaches

Plate 73   M Longridge
The 9ft wheelbase pressed steel heavy bogie

Plate 74   M Longridge
The 7ft wheelbase heavy bogie

99

G.W.R. COACH BOGIES

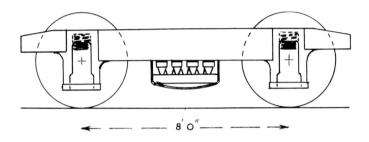

8' 0"

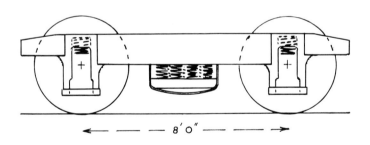

8' 0"

Scale 7mm : 1ft.

Fig 19
Used under Siphon F Diagram O.7

J E D Binney

G.W.R. COACH BOGIES

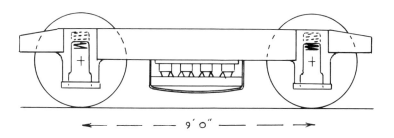

9' 0"

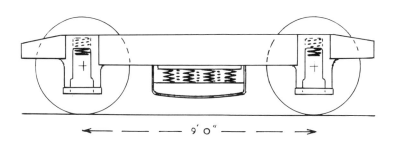

9' 0"

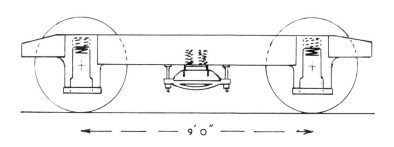

9' 0"

Scale 7mm : 1ft.

Fig 20
Used under Siphon G and Siphon H Diagrams O.11 and O.12

J E D Binney

G.W.R. COACH BOGIES

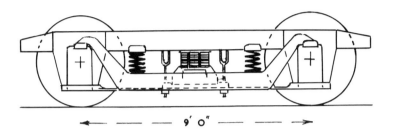

9' 0"

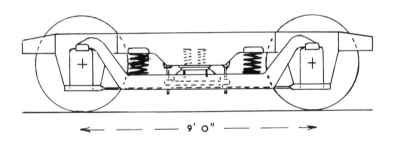

9' 0"

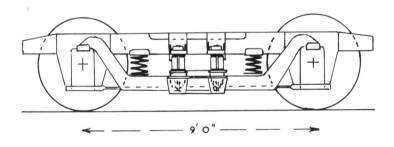

9' 0"

Scale 7mm : 1ft.

Fig 21   J E D Binney
Used under Siphon G, Siphon H and Siphon J Diagrams O.10, O.11, O.12, O.22 and O.31

G.W.R.COACH BOGIES

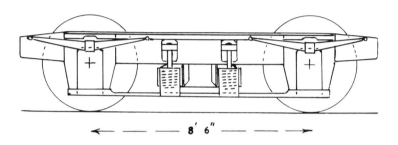

← — — — 8' 6" — — — →

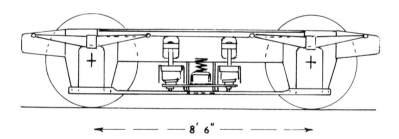

← — — — 8' 6" — — — →

Scale 7mm : 1ft.

Fig 22   J E D Binney
These are the ex-articulated stock bogies and were used under Siphon G Diagrams O.33, O.59 and M.34

G.W.R. COACH BOGIES

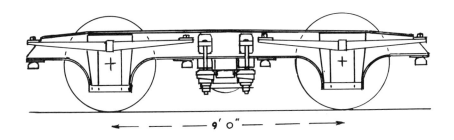

9' 0"

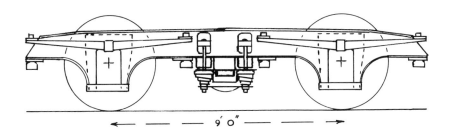

9' 0"

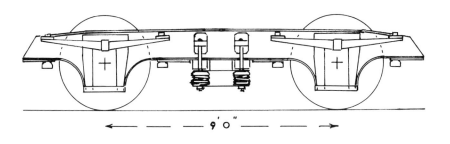

9' 0"

Scale 7mm : 1ft.

Fig 23   **J E D Binney**
Used under Siphon G Diagrams O.33, O.59, O.62 and M.34 and Siphon J Diagram O.40

G.W.R. COACH BOGIES

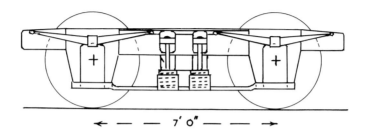

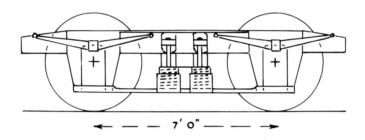

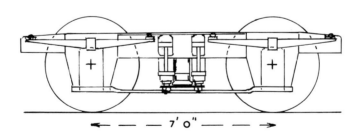

Scale 7mm : 1ft.

Fig 24   J E D Binney
Used under Siphon G Diagrams O.10, O.11 and O.22 and Siphon J Diagram O.31

Diagram O.13

Although not Siphons these four vans merit a mention as being the only vans other than Siphons built expressly for milk traffic. They were designated as "Milk Train Brake Vans" and carried the legend "Milk Train Brake Van to and from London" permanently painted on the side.

Their origins were Pharmacy Cars used in ambulance service overseas during the 1914-18 war and it is assumed they were built specifically for that purpose as no other trace of their origins can be found. It is not believed that they arose from the re-building of two toplight carriages also bought back from war service at the same time.

The Company did not perpetuate the practice of special building of Milk Train brakes but used mostly four and six wheel PBVs until they were withdrawn followed by 40ft vans and later steel panelled 57ft vans suitably branded. Each section of any milk train which was for a different destination had to have its own brake van.

Plate 75   NUVB
The purpose built milk train brake van No 1397 as originally constructed

106

LOT 1299

Built	No	Cond ex Pharmacy Car No	
11/21	1397	4/59	39033
	1398	2/61	39034
	1399	10/59	39035
	1400		39036

NOTES

No 1400 was transferred to ED use as No 14060 in 2/48 as Mess van and is now preserved on the Severn Valley Railway

Other brandings

No 1397 Faringdon & Cricklewood 3/38
       Frome & Cricklewood 8/37
       Ealing & Cricklewood 2/40

No 1399 Lavington & Cricklewood 10/31
       Frome & Cricklewood 5/37

No 1400 Return to Stratford on Avon 5/47

No 1399 is preserved on the Severn Valley Railway

Plate 76   M Longridge
Milk train brake van No W 1399 with ends rebuilt with steel panels. Early BR crimson livery with yellow lettering

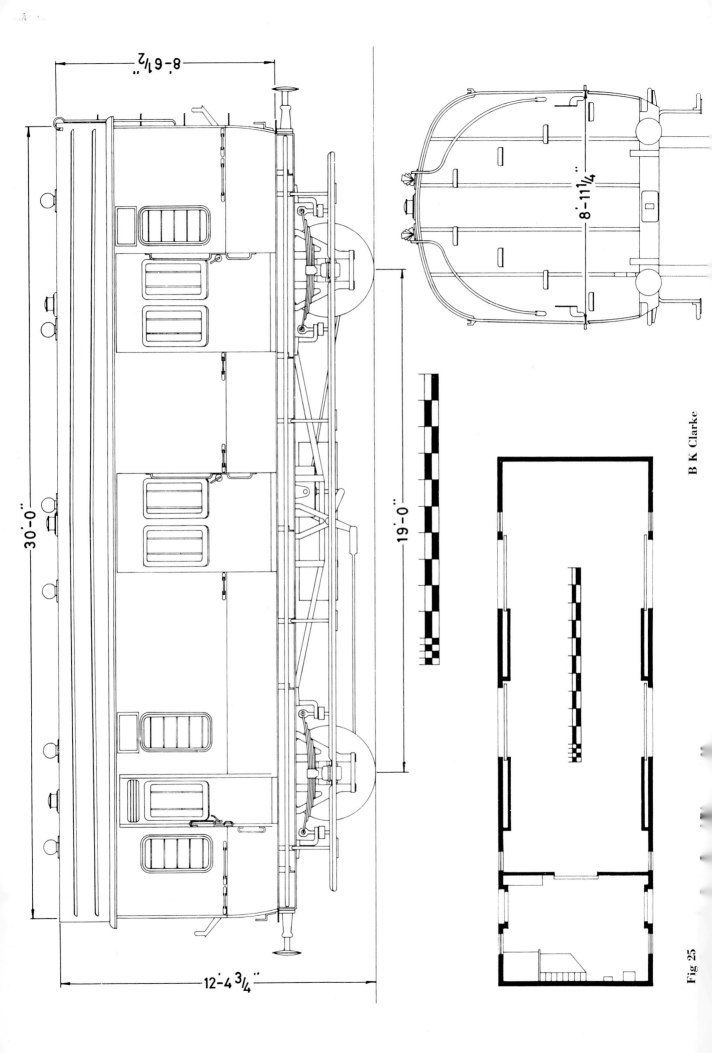

8'-6¹⁄₂"

30'-0"

8'-11¹⁄₄"

19'-0"

12'-4³⁄₄"

B K Clarke

Fig 25

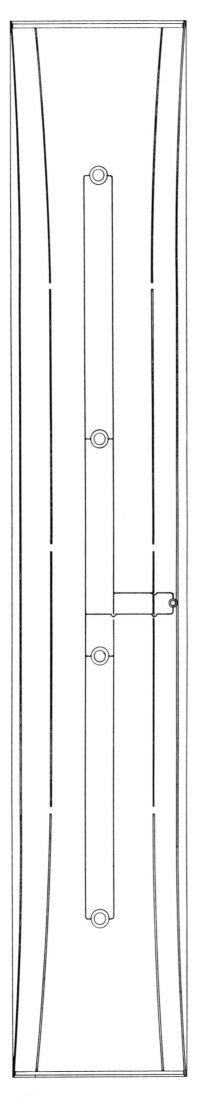

B K Clarke

Fig 26
The gas pipe arrangements on the roof of Siphon G

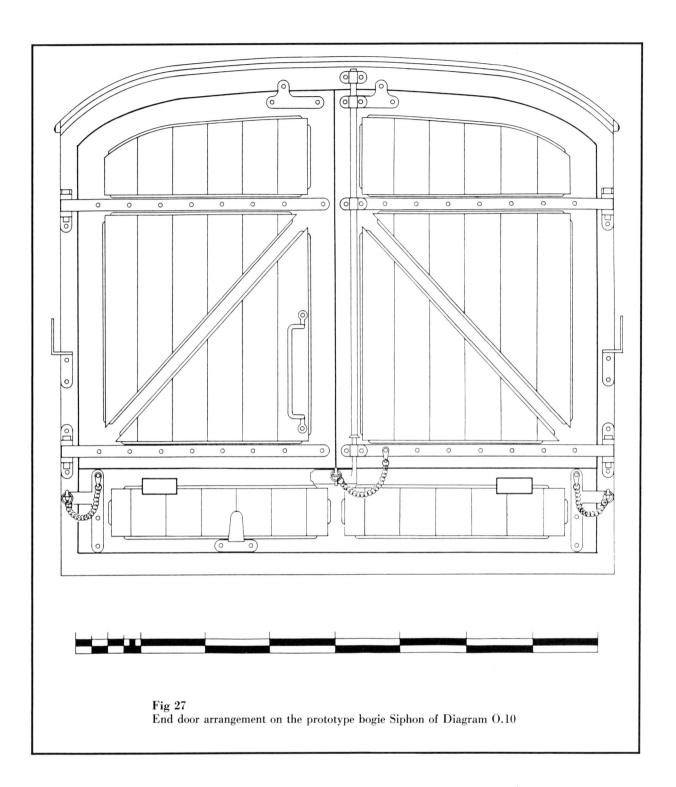

Fig 27
End door arrangement on the prototype bogie Siphon of Diagram O.10

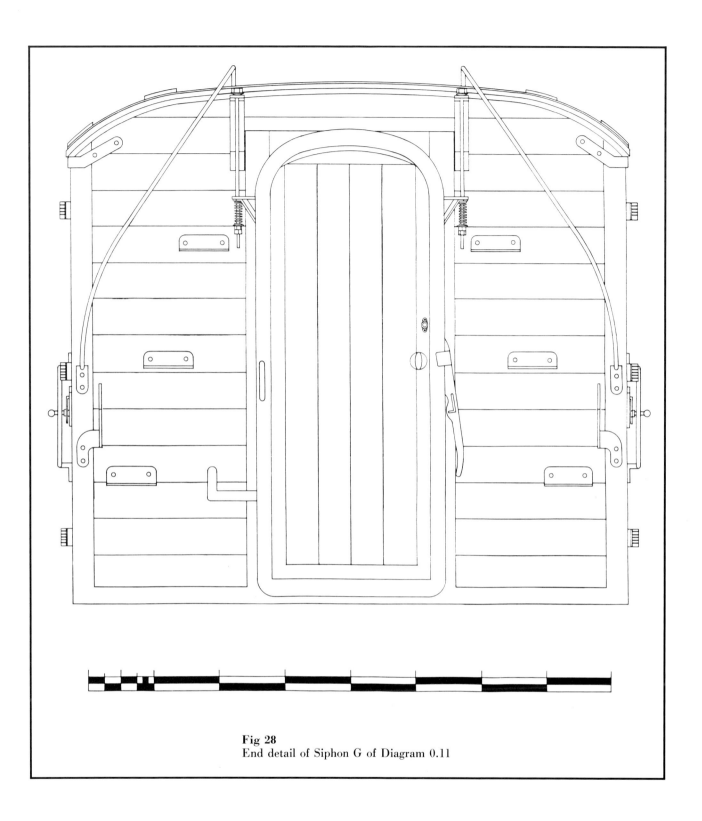

Fig 28
End detail of Siphon G of Diagram 0.11

111

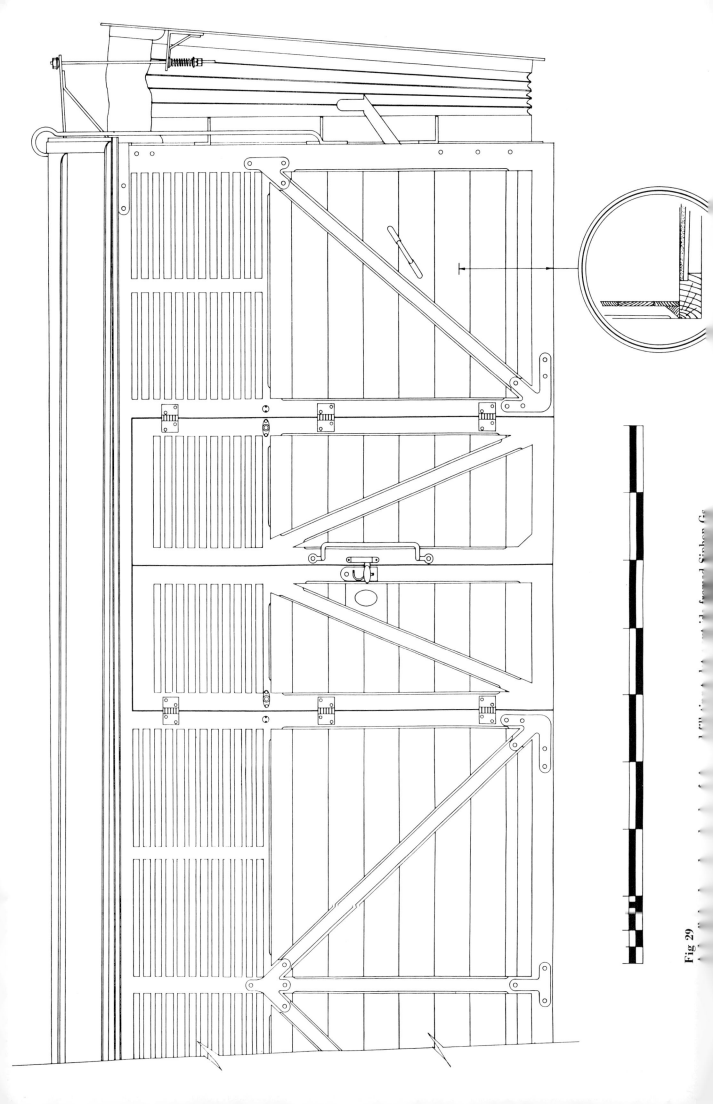

Fig 29

Appendix I

Broad Gauge vehicles converted for Milk Traffic
ex-Vale of Neath Railway Third Class carriages

V of N Third No	G.W.R. Third No	To Milk Van	G.W.R. Van No	Cond	
21	132	4/70	166	11/87	Iron bodies and iron
22	133	4/70	167	5/87	frames. 27ft × 4in × 9ft
24	135	7/70	168	10/87	9in; 6 × 4ft wheels 18ft 4in wheelbase.

The above were converted at Paddington but re-numbered into the van list at Newton Abbot.

ex-Carriage Trucks

Built	G.W.T. CT No	To Milk Van	Cond	
2/56	15		5/86	Wood bodies and wood
11/57	22	8/77	9/91	frames; No dimensions
5/57	25	3/77	9/90	survive except 4 × 4ft
7/55	67	11/77	3/82	wheels. These retained
6/55	106	7/77	9/90	their carriage truck numbers and were fitted with hoops to carry tar- paulin covers.

ex-Vans

Built	G.W.R. Van No	To Milk Van	Cond	
8/52	55	10/77	8/87	Iron bodies and iron
8/52	56	9/77	4/90	frames. 27ft 4in × 9ft 9in; 6 × 4ft wheels 18ft 4in wheelbase. Built Vulcan Foundry.

Appendix II

Modellers, in particular, may be interested in the dates that either side brakes were fitted to the 6 wheel Siphons. The following are specimen dates for various Lots and include earliest and latest fittings. Almost all such brakes had been removed by late 1936

LOT 710	1951	9/09	LOT 741	1902	6/09	LOT 770	1892	7/11
	1955	4/13		1903	11/14		1891	2/13
	1958	11/20		1913	1/32		1899	3/15

LOT 788	1879	4/08	LOT 800	1878	5/08	LOT 822	1865	4/08
	1883	2/10		1873	12/14		1860	2/15
	1881	1/13		1877	12/15		1868	9/19

LOT 825	1853	10/09	LOT 835	1845	1/09	LOT 856	1799	10/12
	1858	4/11		1851	8/10		1802	1/13
	1857	12/11		1848	9/18		1793	10/18

LOT 848	1823	5/09	LOT 857	1818	4/09	LOT 868	1803	5/08
	1828	11/11		1813	5/13		1812	2/10
	1824	11/15		1815	5/19		1807	7/16

LOT 886	1783	1/09	LOT 942	1775	2/09	LOT 943	1739	2/08
	1790	12/12		1778	12/12		1748	3/10
	1785	8/18		1773	2/16		1747	9/18

LOT 951	1772	5/09	LOT 961	1724	4/08	LOT 979	1714	2/09
	1753	1/11		1722	4/10		1709	10/11
	1765	1/15		1726	5/18		1716	8/21

LOT 993	1695	4/08	LOT 997	1682	2/08	LOT 1016	1660	2/08
	1697	9/15		1664	6/12		1649	3/14
	1700	2/17		1668	10/18		1654	4/21

LOT 1034	1642	9/08	LOT 1039	1613	4/08	LOT 1044	1606	4/08
	1637	5/12		1633	1/12		1564	11/11
	1640	11/16		1624	9/14		1598	10/15

LOT 1082	1549	11/08
	1558	12/08
	1555	11/11

and for SIPHON C:-

LOT 1125	1534	12/08	Remainder built with these brakes
	1538	9/12
	1542	9/12

and for SIPHON F:-

LOT 1124	1544	9/12	LOT 1164	1502	10/12
	1545	1/14			

NOTE
The Siphon Cs and Siphon F's did not have these brakes removed.

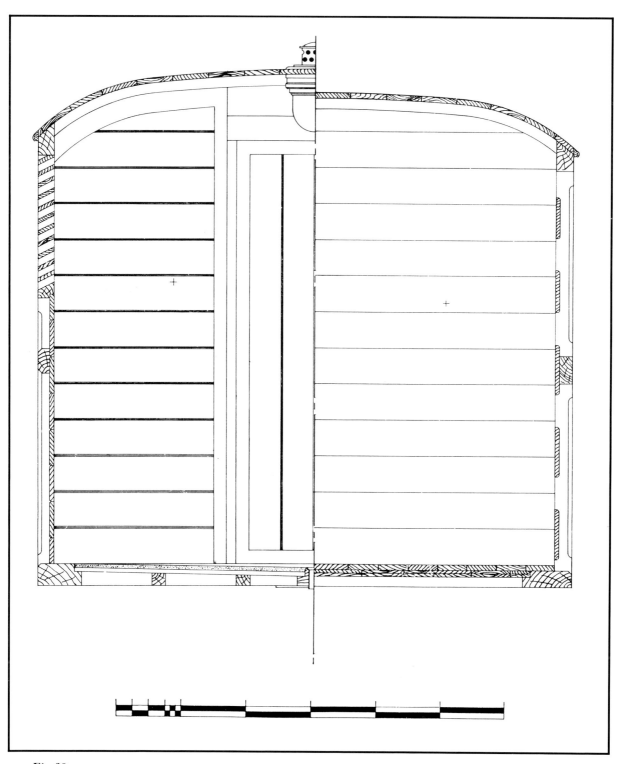

Fig 30   **B K Clarke**
A sectional diagram to shew the arrangement of louvres and planks of Diagram O.11 (left hand side) and the
planks and gaps on the sides of Diagram O.5 (right hand side)

Appendix III

AMBULANCE TRAIN FORMATIONS

The trains for which Siphon Gs were provided were numbered 32-35/45/46 and each vehicle was numbered from 1-14 within each train prefixed by the train number, eg 3201, 3213 etc.

Car No	Description	Type	Diag
1	Brake and boiler	BTK	D 118
2-5	Ward cars	Siphon G	O 33
6	Pharmacy car	BTK	D 118
7-9	Ward cars	Siphon G	O 33
10	Sitting up cases	TK	C 68
11	Kitchen	Restaurant	H 16
12	Staff	LMS Sleeper	
13	Nurses	LMS Sleeper	
14	Stores and office	BTK	D 94

The actual trains were made up of the vehicles whose serial numbers are given below in the order of types above:

Train No	Vehicles
32	5989, 2789, 2759, 2768, 2774, 5803, 2782, 2776, 2799, 4568, 9548, , , 4763
33	5993, 2792, 2790, 2798, 2778, 5805, 2783, 2752, 2754, 4563, 9549, 503, 528, 4761
34	5884, 2064, 2757, 2761, 2763, 5804, 2765, 2767, 2771, 4567, 9551, 548, 551, 4765
35	5983, 2751, 2755, 2756, 2758, 5807, 2766, 2069, 2794, 4569, 9546, 559, 569, 4751
45	5885, 2760, 2068, 2793, 2770, 5806, 2061, 2062, 2775, 4564, 9550, 561, 578, 4753
46	5988, 2063, 2760, 2769, 2784, 5880, 2786, 2781, 2791, 4570, 9547, 570, 564, 4759

The following Siphon Gs were used in two ambulance trains for the US Army:

69   Nos 2979-2984

70   Nos 2777/2926-8/30/78

And the remainder of the Casualty Evacuation Train Siphon Gs were returned to traffic as Diagram O.59:

Nos 2066/7/70/2762-3/79-80/85/7/8/95-7/2800

Conversions to ambulance duty were made in 1943/4 and the vans were re-converted to ordinary traffic in 1945/6

Appendix IV

LOADS and TARES
Particularly for the benefit of modellers and others involved in painting the following notes are given of representative loads and tares. The loads are correct from Swindon ¼in Diagrams except for that for the original 4 wheel Siphon for which no authoritative source has been found. The estimate given is based on contemporary practice for vans of similar dimensions. It is known that with original springing the load was 4 or 5T.

Loads
4 wheel Siphon original Diagram O.1	7T
6 wheel Siphons Diagrams O.1 to O.6	10T
4 wheel Siphon C Diagrams O.8 and O.9	10T
8 wheel Siphon F Diagram O.7	18T
8 wheel Siphons G, H, Diagrams O.10, O.11, O.12, O.22, O.33, O.59 and O.62	14T
8 wheel Siphon J Diagram O.31	15T
8 wheel Siphon J Diagram O.40	12T
8 wheel parcels van Diagram M.34	14T

Tare Weights

4 whl			6 whl			
O.1	O.1	O.2	O.3	O.4	O.5	O.6
6.13	10.7	10.6	10.5	10.11	10.17	10.13

		4 whl				
		O.8		O.9		
		10.14		11.4		

		8 whl				
O.7	O.10	O.11	O.12	O.22	O.31	O.40
22.7	25.11	25.17	23.15	25.10	26.13	26.12

Plate 77
Empty Siphons being marshalled at Paddington for return to the West Country

HMRS

O.33	9ft heavy bogies	25.17
	8ft 6in single bolster bogies	28.6
	8ft 6in double bolster bogies	29.7
	other bogies	25.16
O.59	7ft bogies	25.13
	9ft bogies	25.17
	8ft 6in single bolster bogies	28.6
	8ft 6in double bolster bogies	29.7
O.62	9ft American bogies	27.4
	7ft heavy bogies	26.9
	9ft heavy bogies	26.6
M.34	7ft bogies	25.13
	9ft bogies	25.17

Appendix V

CONSTRUCTIONAL DETAILS

The following details have been collected together in this Appendix to avoid stereotyped repetition in several sections of the book of the same information.

Buffers

Round buffers were the norm for early Siphons and the Siphon F were the first type to receive oval buffers in 1912. These were carried in the standard square tapered body. The prototype end door "Siphon G" also had the oval buffers and the outside framed Siphon G to Diagram O.11 followed suit. All such fittings were replaced by large round head coach buffers by 1938.

Door Hand Holes

Also in 1912 holes were made in doors of Siphon F to enable the catches to be easily reached. No 1546 had oval holes but Nos 1547 and 1548 had square and smaller ones which were identical to those on Siphon C. Photographs shew these clearly.

Outside Framing

The outside framing of Siphons C and F was chamfered on its top edge to encourage the dispersal of rain water and the practice continued with Siphon H and the early Lots of Siphon G. Later only the framing of the doors was so treated and in even later years a fillet of wood along the bottom rail of the sides replaced the chamfering. In the last outside framed designs a small triangular corner piece was inserted in the door framing both to repel water and add strength.

119

Plate 78
2—6—0 No 9317 with both old and new milk vans

J Craig

Westinghouse Brakes
All Westinghouse brake fittings were removed from all types of Siphon by the early 1930s. The underfloor pipes went straight through so that the Westinghouse flexible pipe at one end was to the left of the vacuum pipe and to the right of it at the other end.

Underframes
In Multibar trussing the Queen posts were "L" angles $3\frac{1}{2}$in $\times$ $3\frac{1}{2}$in and the central horizontal bars $1\frac{1}{4}$in diam. Both the end sloping bars and the cross bars were $1\frac{3}{4}$in diam.

Acknowledgements

The genesis from which this book sprang was in a period of research which I was privileged to undertake in the Drawing Office at Swindon. Here H J Ridout and his colleague Rowland Jones went to great trouble to find information for me and always made me welcome. At about the same time the Swindon branch of the National Union of Vehicle Builders provided me with a copy of the photograph of each of the vehicles their members had worked on.

Gaps in those records have been filled since those far off days through the willing cooperation of T J Edgington and his colleagues at York Museum and, more particularly, the disposal dates between 1960 and 1985 by the kindness and industry of Chris Darrall.

Departmental stock records from Lineside Publications and Platform Five proved useful while the records of D M Lee, J H Lewis and the late J E D Binney all revealed snippets that were used.

Finally David Hyde volunteered to check the typescript but went far beyond the call of duty and produced a good deal of detail information from his own research which made the text more complete. My thanks to all of these good friends.

4—4—0 No 3330 on a train with the first van of Diagram O.5

THE HMRS

About the publishers of this book

The Historical Model Railway Society is a charitable educational Trust, celebrating its 35th Anniversary in 1985. The Society has certain clearly defined objectives and its primary concern has been to foster the research and recording of information relating to the railways of the British Isles, and to ensure that this information is disseminated widely, and in particular for the benefit of model makers to help them build accurate and authentic models. The Society has over 1700 members world wide and they comprise not only active researchers and model makers but also those simply with a broad affection for Britain's railway heritage.

The Society has an active publications policy and this is a key way to ensuring that the fruits of members' research are passed on to a wide audience. The Society has made a particular study of liveries, recognising that this aspect, though of considerable importance to model makers, has often been poorly recorded. Earlier livery registers have dealt with the Caledonian, London & South Western, Southern, Midland and Great Western Railways. The Society also publishes a high quality quarterly Journal and a regular Newsletter both of which are distributed free to members. The Society's activities encompass all periods of railway history, and whilst at first it was primarily concerned with the recording of the pre-grouping scene today both the grouped companies and British Railways have strong followings within its membership.

The Society has extensive collections of drawings and photographs, which are particularly strong in their coverage of carriages and wagons, as well as an extensive library. Information is also circulated through a system of Company Stewards, each specialising in a particular company and acting as a clearing house for the exchange of informtion, so that members with a particular interest in one company have a definite point of contact for information and inquiries. There are also local area groups meeting regularly in different parts of the country.

Further information and a membership prospectus is available from:
P.A.Ray,Hon.Membership Secretary,
7 Field Style Road, SOUTHWOLD, Suffolk, IP18 6LA.